# THE MIRROR OF ALCHEMY

Eamus Quesitum Quatuor Elementorum naturas

*Gareth Roberts*

# The Mirror of Alchemy

Alchemical Ideas and Images in Manuscripts and Books

*from Antiquity to the Seventeenth Century*

UNIVERSITY OF TORONTO PRESS
TORONTO BUFFALO

*(frontispiece): An alchemist with a flask and a scroll which reads* Eamus Quesitum Quasuor Elemementorum [sic, *ie* Quattuor Elementorum] Naturas *(Let us go in search of the natures of the four elements). Solomon Trismosin,* Splendor solis *(1582).*
[BL, Harley MS 3469, f.4]

© 1994 Gareth Roberts
Published in North America by
University of Toronto Press Incorporated

First published 1994 by
The British Library
Great Russell Street
London WC1B 3DG

Canadian Cataloguing in Publication Data

Roberts, Gareth, 1949–
    The mirror of alchemy

Co-published by the British Library.
Includes bibliographical reference and index.
ISBN 0–8020–0710–4 (bound). – ISBN 0–8020–7660–2 (pbk.)

1. Alchemy – Europe – Early works to 1800.
2. British Library – Catalogs. I. British Library.
II. Title.

QD13.R63 1994    540'.1'12094        C94–932320–9

ISBN 0–8020–0710–4 (hardback)
     0–8020–7660–2 (paperback)

Designed by Andrew Shoolbred
Typeset by August Filmsetting, Haydock, St Helens
Printed in England by Henry Ling (Printers) Ltd,
Dorchester, Dorset

# CONTENTS

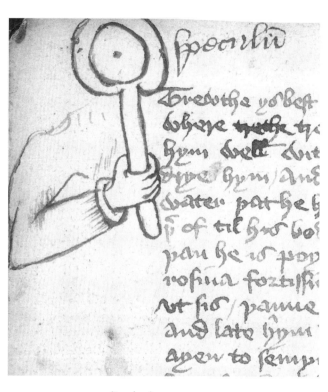

*'Speculum.'*
[BL, Sloane MS 976, f.84v]

# PREFACE

Scholastic philosophy with its infinitely subtle arguments, theology with its ambiguous phraseology, astrology – so vast and complicated – are only child's play compared with alchemy.

Albert Poisson, *Théories et symboles des alchimistes*

The history of an error.

Robert Halleux, *Les textes alchimiques*

This book has two main goals. In its attempt to describe and explain some of the history and basic concepts, terms, and presuppositions of western European alchemy it aims to provide the reader with a 'primer' or introduction to alchemy. It does this through illustration from alchemical writings from the third to the seventeenth centuries, particularly from the highly metaphorical language and the visual images of alchemy, and focuses on material from the fifteenth to seventeenth centuries, when the production and transmission of alchemical texts were at their height. Alchemy's theories and iconography inform the thought, literature and the visual arts of the middle ages and the Renaissance; some of its ideas survived into the eighteenth century; and in the twentieth century C G Jung found its images like the language of the unconscious. Geoffrey Chaucer, John Donne and Ben Jonson were particularly well-versed in alchemy, and some of its operations and technicalities were sufficiently commonplace for Shakespeare's sonnets to refer in passing to the morning sun 'Gilding pale streams with heavenly alchemy' (sonnet 33.4), and a faithless woman's deceiving tears having been 'Distilled from limbecks [alembics*] foul as hell within' (sonnet 119.2).

*Words or phrases marked on their first appearance with an asterisk (*) will be found explained in the Glossary of Alchemical Terms at the end of the book (pp.97–113).

1 For example, *Auriferae artis, quam chemiam vocant* (Basle 1572) contains, one after another (1–69, 71–151) two different rescensions of what is probably one of the earliest alchemical texts in Latin, the *Turba philosophorum*. On the *Turba*, *see below* Chapter I, pp.26–7.

All the quotations in this book, and its visual illustrations, are taken from the particularly rich collections of alchemical manuscripts and books in The British Library. British Library pressmarks are provided for all the books and manuscripts from which colour and black-and-white illustrations are taken.

A few preliminary remarks and caveats are necessary. There are a dauntingly vast number of alchemical texts, and this book refers to only a very few. And there are even problems in referring to an alchemical 'text', as alchemical works in manuscript were often modified, abridged, added to and changed in the course of their transmission.[1] Sometimes commentaries on the original text were added to alchemical manuscripts in a way which rendered

2 Halleux 1979: 7. On all these problems of alchemical texts, *see also* Thorndike 1923–58: iii 39–43.

them difficult to distinguish from the 'original' text. The titles of treatises are also liable to change, or the same treatises may exist under two or more titles, or the same title may refer to a number of quite different treatises: there are many alchemical 'Rosaries' and 'Flowers'. The editing, examination and study of alchemical texts, in the form of both manuscripts and early printed books, has hardly begun. In the words of Robert Halleux, 'l'immense masse des textes alchimiques attend ses prospecteurs, ses éditeurs et ses exégètes'.[2] Historiographically, part of the reason for this is that, like the history of witchcraft, there are senses in which the history of alchemy is 'the history of an error', and some historians of science regarded alchemy as an unfortunate dream from which chemistry fortunately struggled awake. It is not just that alchemy, as it was understood, could not produce gold from lead, and that the alchemist's understanding of the material world is not that of modern science; the names of substances and processes in alchemical texts do not necessarily refer to those substances and processes now bearing those names. '*Aes*' (usually translated 'bronze') could mean a variety of substances that were bright, heavy and a certain colour: 'aes doth not alwaies signifie

3 Dorn 1650: sig. Aaav.

Copper, but sometimes Gold, or Silver, or any other Metall …'.[3] 'Gold', 'bronze' and 'copper' mean different things at different times in history, and it is impossible to say that there is any one fixed meaning to the names of substances commonly mentioned in alchemy such as minium, nitrum, sal ammoniac, calx and vitriol.[4] An entry in a modern dictionary for 'magnesia'

4 *See* Crosland 1962: 104–10.

will show that there might still be some doubt about what exactly is meant by the use of the word in the twentieth century, but magnesium oxide (chemical formula $MgO$) would probably be intended. But if at any time up to the seventeenth century one were to ask Chaucer's Canon's Yeoman's ques-

5 *See* 'Canon's Yeoman's tale' in Chaucer 1957: 222 line 1458.
6 For example, in *Hydrolicus Sophicus* in *Musaeum Hermeticum* 1678: 84.

tion, 'What is Magnasia, good sire, I yow preye?'[5] then there would be all sorts of different answers, including the use of 'universal magnesia' (*magnesium quoque Catholicam*) as a periphrasis for the Philosophers' Stone itself.[6] And alchemists' love of metaphor, enigma, allegory and riddle often means that the normal modes of alchemical discourse are figurative not literal. Alchemical texts are difficult to understand even when they attempt to speak clearly, let alone when they express a succession of processes as a vulture flying without wings and crying on top of the mountain, 'I am the white of the blacke, and the red of the white, and the Citrine sonne of the

7 Artephius 1624: 194.

red'.[7] And in many cases the name of the author claimed for an alchemical treatise is incorrect. This may be obvious in the case of Moses, or Miriam his sister, Aristotle or Thrice-Great Hermes, less so in the cases of (say) Avicenna or of Ramon Lull. Readers of this book are therefore advised, when they come across the name of an author of a treatise on alchemy, mentally to put inverted commas around such names as 'Albertus Magnus' or 'Arnold of Villanova'.

Short references in the notes will be found expanded in the Bibliography of texts cited at the end of the book (pp.115–8). I have not cited particular editions of some standard texts, for example works of classical literature and the Bible. Unless otherwise indicated, all translations are my own.

# Acknowledgements

My thanks are due to colleagues in the Classics Department in Exeter, especially Dave Braund, Chris Gill and Richard Seaford for their willingness to accompany me through some very unclassical Greek in early alchemical texts, and to Peter Wiseman for his continuing patience with requests to look over some of my translations from Latin. I am grateful to Lawrence Normand for reading drafts of chapters.

Some of the research for this book was done during study leave granted me by the University of Exeter whose Research Committee also awarded me a grant towards work on this book. The rest was done in the course of a year's temporary lectureship at King's College London. I am grateful to King's for appointing me for a year and particularly to my colleagues in the English Department where I spent a very happy and productive year, and to Exeter for granting me a year's leave of absence to take up the post. Work on the later stages of the alchemical operation was hastened by the award of a fellowship from the Centre for the Book at The British Library. My thanks also to Anne Young of British Library Publications for supervising the production of this book, and particularly to Jane Carr for her kindness and courtesy, and her graceful amalgam of tact and encouragement, especially at those moments when projection seemed slow in arriving.

*Gareth Roberts*
*February 1994*

# LIST OF COLOUR PLATES

Seminate aurum veftrum in terram albam foliatam.

# EPIGRAMMA VI.

R Uricolæ pingui mandant fua femina terræ,
  Cùm fuerit raftris hæc foliata fuis.
Philofophi niveos aurum docuère per agros
  Spargere, qui folii fe levis inftar habent :
Hoc ut agas, illud bene refpice, namque quod aurum
  Germinet, ex tritico videris, ut fpeculo.

                                    E        PLATO

*Fig. 1 'Sow your gold in white foliated earth'. Michael Maier,* Atalanta fugiens *(Oppenheim 1617).*

[BL, 90.i.19, Emblem VI, p.33]

CHAPTER 1

# ORIGINS, BEGINNINGS AND EARLY HISTORIES

Will you believe antiquity? Records?
I'll show you a book, where Moses, and his sister,
And Solomon have written, of the art;
Ay, and a treatise penned by Adam.

Ben Jonson, *The alchemist*

... in the Bible some can finde out Alchimy.

John Donne, 'A valediction: of the booke'

1 Debus 1965: 24–6.

If we believe the alchemists themselves, their art had an antiquity literally as old as Adam, or even older. For the sixteenth-century followers of the Swiss physician and alchemist Paracelsus (c.1493–1541), creation itself was an event in which 'the great workemaister and Creator' distinguished light and darkness, and more especially divided first the firmament and then dry land from the waters in divine acts of alchemical separation*.[1] For the seventeenth-century alchemist Sendivogius, the earth is a great distilling vessel formed by the Creator.[2] The *Turba philosophorum* also speaks of the Creator engaged in acts of coagulation* and commingling.[3]

2 Coudert 1980: 80.

3 *Turba* tr Waite 1896: 25.

4 Eliade 1962: 190–1.

At the other end of time, the fires essential to the alchemical processes prefigured the conflagrations and purifications to come at the Last Judgement, not just to the alchemists but also to Martin Luther.[4] And at the turning-point in between, in a Christian programme of history, so John Donne wrote, Christ after his death had figuratively

For these three daies become a minerall;
Hee was all gold when he lay downe, but rose
All tincture*, ...[5]

5 John Donne, 'Resurrection, imperfect', in Donne 1962: 28 lines 12–14.

6 *Gloria mundi* cited in Coudert 1980: 195.

7 Robert Bostocke, *Difference betwene the auncient Phisicke ... and the latter Phisicke* (1585) quoted in Debus 1962: 5.

In Eden before the Fall Adam was thought to have possessed an unique knowledge of the wonderful secrets of nature, including that of the Philosophers' Stone, which may have accounted for his longevity:[6] he died aged 930. At the very least Adam was thought to have been 'indowed with singular knowledge, wisdom and light of nature'[7]. This made him the first and most knowledgeable alchemical adept. This history of alchemy is similar to other mythic constructions in western culture of a golden age of knowledge, religion, science, poetry or music: knowledge was always perfect or at least fuller or more pristine in the distant past. The title of one of the alchemical

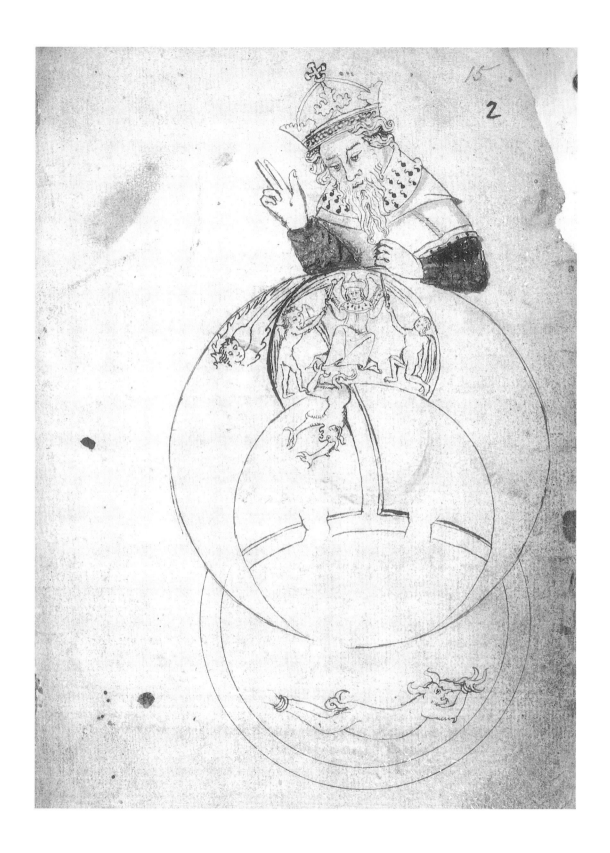

ORIGINS, BEGINNINGS AND EARLY HISTORIES

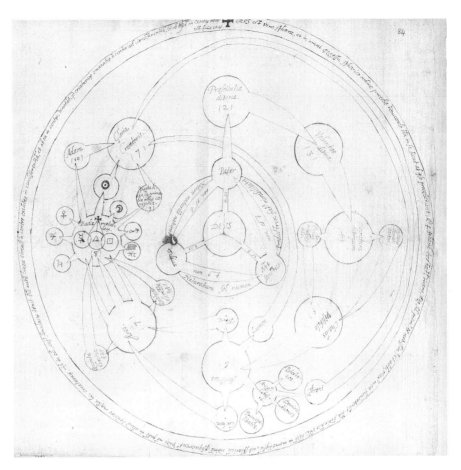

Fig. 2 (opposite) *God supervises his Creation and Satan falls from heaven. A drawing in a miscellaneous collection of alchemical works.* See also *the engraving in Elias Ashmole,* Theatrum chemicum Britannicum *(1652) [BL, G.18,920, p.210].*

[BL, Egerton MS 845, f.15.]

Fig. 3 *A sixteenth-century circular diagram representing some aspects of Creation, prefatory to an alchemical treatise in English. A note on the back of the diagram (f.83) describes it as 'Liber naturae sive Chaos veterum Generalem metallorum generationem &c demonstrans' (The book of Nature, or the Chaos of the ancients, showing the general generation of metals etc). In the middle of the diagram is God in the Trinity. From him proceeds a series of numbered divine manifestations, such as Divine Presence (2), the Divine Will (3) and the Creator's Glory (7). On the left, the eighth circle contains* Radix metallorum *(the root of metals), mercury, sulphur and salt (see below, Chapter 3, p.51), represented by their usual symbols, which in turn generate the seven metals, represented by their usual planetary symbols. Gold or the sun has a special position, being generated by both the root of metals and also directly as a result of the Creator's Glory*

[BL, Sloane MS 1198, ff.83v–84.]

8 *Musaeum Hermeticum* 1678: 53–72.

treatises printed in the seventeenth-century collection *Musaeum Hermeticum* (1678) is *Aureum seculum redivivum* ('The Golden Age Returned').[8] This idea persisted in medieval and early modern western culture and was revived by the Renaissance. Later alchemy was largely an attempt to recover an understanding now fragmented, uncertain and imperfect since a time in a distant past: before the Fall Adam 'knewe the natures and properties of things better than we'.[9] Alchemy looked back: the ancients possessed the secrets of an art which later alchemists tried to recover partly through deciphering the texts of their predecessors. In such origins as these for alchemy, and in such uses of alchemical analogies for Christian doctrine and history (*see below*, Chapter 4, pp. 78–82), alchemists made a claim for the art's antiquity and also for the legitimacy of its knowledge and practices. This claim was often made in the awareness that another body of opinion saw knowledge, especially 'curious' learning, science and technology, as having at least highly suspicious ancient origins, sometimes indeed as dubious arts taught to fallen mankind by demons before the Flood, rather than as remnants of a pre-lapsarian plenitude and perfection of knowledge. Among early Christian writers of approximately the same era as the earliest alchemical documents, Clement of Alexandria (*c*.150–*c*.213) and Tertullian (*c*.155–*c*.220), held the view that fallen angels had instructed mankind in such techniques as metal-working, interpretation of the stars and magic.[10] One of the earliest extant alchemical writers, Zosimos of Panopolis (?third century AD) is cited as saying much the same thing. In another very early alchemical text, Isis tells her son Horus that the angel Amnäel taught her alchemical techniques after overtures of sex.[11] Both views of alchemy persisted in its later history: a holy and pious art analogous to God's own creation and to his subsequent supervision of nature and also to the most sacred mysteries of faith; or an art of dubious authority that vainly presumed to imitate divine acts of making and changing proper only to God. The English Puritan William Perkins was not alone in arguing that the alchemical attempt to change other metals into gold is

9 Debus 1962: 5. Cf Luther, 'We are beginning to regain a knowledge of the creation, a knowledge we had forfeited by the fall of Adam', quoted by Montgomery 1963: 255.

10 Berthelot 1885: 9–20. *See also* Thorndike 1923–58: i 436–79 and Carlo Ginzburg, 'The high and the low: the theme of forbidden knowledge in the sixteenth and seventeenth centuries' in Ginzburg 1990: 60–76.

11 Berthelot 1888: ii 28–33 and iii 31–36.

> a thing in trueth unpossible: for it is a kinde of newe creation, to turne one kind of creature into a creature of another kinde, as every metall is. And that which is said or rather dreamed of the Philosopher's stone, is but a conceit, and no where to be found, but in *Utopia*.[12]

12 William Perkins, *A treatise of callings*, in *Works*, Cambridge 1603: 920–1.

As successors to Adam as the founding father of the art, alchemists claimed a host of venerable authorities who practised alchemy or wrote alchemical works. The thirteenth-century encyclopaedist Vincent of Beauvais begins his list of alchemists with Adam and Noah.[13] Among the Old Testament patriarchs and prophets, Noah, Moses, David and Solomon supposedly knew the art, and it was revealed to Enoch in a vision. Among the ancient Greek philosophers, Pythagoras, Socrates, Plato and Aristotle testified to it; Homer, Virgil and Ovid among classical poets. Among the apostles, St John the Evangelist was an alchemist, among the theologians John Damascene, Albertus Magnus and his pupil St Thomas Aquinas. Elias Ashmole thought

13 Vincent of Beauvais 1624: VII lxxxvii col. 480. *See also* Patai 1983.

PLATE I *God creates the world. Pen and watercolour drawing, 'Cabala mineralis Rabbi Simon Ben Cantara'.*
*[BL, Additional MS 5245, f.8.]*

PLATE II *(overleaf) An alchemical disciple receives a book from his master. The kneeling figure may be intended to represent Norton.* Thomas Norton, Ordinal of alchemy.
*[BL, Additional MS 10,302, f.6v.]*

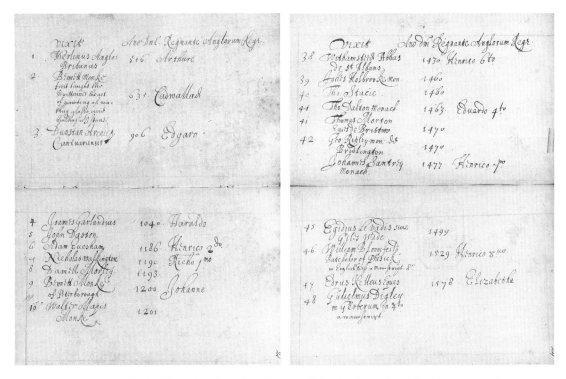

*Fig. 4 'A Lookeing Glasse for Illitterate Alchymists'. The list of British alchemists begins with Merlin and includes St Dunstan, George Ripley and Edward Kelley.*

[BL, Sloane MS 2218, ff.20v–21, 23v–24.]

14 Ashmole 1652: 467.

the 'Canon Yeoman's Tale' showed Chaucer to be a master of the art.[14] Just as alchemists claimed distinguished ancient figures as legitimising predecessors, so alchemical works apocryphally fathered themselves upon venerable authors. Moses, partly because he 'was learned in all the wisdom of the Egyptians' (Acts 7:22) is already cited as an alchemical authority in third-century Greek papyri at Leiden.[15] In an eleventh-century manuscript in St

15 Berthelot 1888: i 9, 16–17.

Mark's Venice, which transcribes Greek works also dating perhaps from the third century AD, Moses is credited with a recipe for doubling the weight of

16 Berthelot 1888: i 61.

gold (St Mark's Venice, Marcianus Graecus 299, f.185)[16]. Albertus Magnus (*c*.1200–1280), the Dominican theologian, philosopher and commentator on Aristotle, is credited with the authorship of alchemical treatises, many represented in manuscripts in The British Library (*see below*, Chapter 2, pp.31–3). Most of the distinguished authors claimed by alchemical treatises had nothing to do with those works going under their names: the Majorcan mystic, missionary and poet Ramon Lull (*c*.1235–1316) most certainly wrote none of

17 On all these authors, *see below*, Chapter II.

the 143 alchemical works at various times attributed to him.[17]

The mythical history of alchemy shares with other mythical histories of arts and sciences a desire to trace succession and continuation in its traditions of knowledge. 'There has ever beene a continued Succession of Philosophers

18 Ashmole 1652: 440.

in all Ages, although the heedlesse world hath seldome taken notice of them', claimed Elias Ashmole.[18] Alchemists' desire to establish the antiquity of their art can be seen in the placing of a history of alchemy by Robertus Vallensis, *De veritate et antiquitate artis chemicae*, as the very first work in the most important printed collection of alchemical treatises in the seventeenth century, Zetzner's *Theatrum chemicum* (1602). Elias Ashmole's 'Prolegomena' to his own English 'theatre of alchemy' *Theatrum chemicum Britannicum* (1652) traces a tradition of antique British learning from the Druids onwards in which to situate his 'English Hermetique philosophers'.[19] A seventeenth-century treatise entitled 'A Lookeing Glasse for Illitterate Alchymists' includes a list of the succession of British alchemists, each with his dates and the monarch's reign in which he lived.

19 Ashmole 1652: sigs A2–B4v.

This concern with a tradition of knowledge and instruction in alchemy is discernible on a micro-level in the motif of alchemical adepts who pass on instruction and secrets to disciples who become 'sons' to their masters.[20] Such filiations arc reported in the fifteenth century in England: George Ripley handed on the Art to 'a Canon of Lichfield' and he in turn to Thomas Daulton. Ripley also handed on the Art to a prior of Bath Abbey who transmitted the secret to Thomas Charnock. A fifteenth-century manuscript of Thomas Norton's *Ordinal of alchemy* shows a disciple, perhaps Norton himself,[21] receiving a book from his master and swearing to 'serve the holy secrets of alchemy', while the Holy Spirit and two angels hover approvingly above in a scene with iconography typical of a miniature depicting the Annunciation or Baptism (*see* PLATE II). Elias Ashmole was 'adopted' by his master, the alchemist William Backhouse, in April 1651.[22] Perhaps this tradition of master–pupil succession (John Gower, said Ashmole, was Chaucer's master in the art[23]) was instrumental in the ascription of alchemical treatises to both Albert the Great and his pupil Thomas Aquinas, or in the formation of the legend that Ramon Lull was converted to alchemy by the Catalan physician Arnold of Villanova (*c*.1235–1316). Chaucer's 'Arnold of the Newe Toun' and Lull were two of the most respected medieval alchemical authorities, but Lull probably wrote none of the alchemical treatises that gave him this reputation and Arnold hardly any, if any at all, of those ascribed to him.

20 On this alchemical succession and adoption, *see* Ashmole 1652: 440–1.

21 Norton 1975: xii.

22 *See* Josten 1949: 1–33.

23 Ashmole 1652: 470.

## Early Greek Alchemy

Evidence of alchemy before, or external to, the earliest Greek alchemical texts is difficult to come by. There may be allusions in the elder Pliny, who like so many ancient authorities had a work on the philosophers' stone foisted on him.[24] His *Natural history* (published *c*.77AD) tells of the fraudulent practices of workers in metal and of the emperor Caligula extracting gold from orpiment.[25] There is a tradition that in 290AD the emperor Diocletian put down a revolt in Egypt and burned the books of those who made gold, but the sources for this report, including the tenth-century lexicographer Suidas,[26] are considerably later than the supposed event. Suidas, like many other

24 Thorndike 1923–58: i 52, fn.3.

25 Thorndike 1923–58: i 81.

26 Suidas 1928–38: iv 804.

authorities, clearly thought of Egypt as the home of alchemical operations. Alchemical texts constantly invoke Egyptian sources: the alchemist Zosimos, writing to his sister, says that the land of Egypt was sustained by metal-workers, and metallurgy was thought of as the monopoly of ancient Egypt. Suidas gives the story about Diocletian in the entry in his dictionary under 'chemeia', which it defines as the 'preparation (kataskeue) of silver and gold'.[27] In its turn chemeia may be derived from Khem, an ancient name for Egypt itself. The word 'alchemy'* is formed by prefixing to chemeia the Arabic definite article al- (as in algebra and alcohol*) and that article indicates that alchemy's immediate origins for medieval Europe were Arabic. The word itself therefore encapsulates the early history of western alchemy before the first known Latin translations of alchemical works from the Arabic in the twelfth century. In the word alchemy we can trace the Arabic transmission to Latin culture of a Greek tradition of an art supposed originally Egyptian.

27 Ibid: iv 804.

Given the paucity of external evidence, any attempt to construct an account of early western alchemy must consequently use the earliest Greek alchemical texts: texts that are pseudonymous, apocryphal and dubious. Some of the earliest extant writings on alchemy attribute themselves to deities: one to the Egyptian goddess Isis, another to the Greek god Hermes, others to Moses or Greek philosophers. Democritus (died c.357BC) had a considerable body of work ascribed to him. But the distinction between mythical and historical persons was less clear in the early years of the Christian era. In the letter to her son Horus, Isis calls herself 'a prophetess' (prophetis) rather than a goddess, and St Augustine was not the only writer in antiquity who talked of Isis as a ruler who educated the Egyptians. It was still possible to believe as late as the seventeenth century that Hermes Trismegistus, one of the candidates for the founding father of alchemy, was a historical person contemporary with Moses.

The earliest alchemical texts are papyri in Greek, some found in a magician's tomb in Thebes, which formed part of a collection of antiquities brought together in the early nineteenth century by a Swedish vice-consul in Alexandria. They were bought in 1828 by the government of the Netherlands and are now at Leiden. Of these, Leiden papyrus X[28] is the most chemical. The other early alchemical works are Greek manuscripts, which were described and transcribed by Marcellin Berthelot at the end of the nineteenth century. The oldest (probably from the eleventh century) and finest is in St Mark's Venice (Marcianus Graecus 299); the others, which are later, are in the Bibliothèque Nationale and other European libraries.[29] Partly because of the similarity of some of their contents to those of the papyri, these manuscripts seem to be transcriptions of what were originally more ancient collections of alchemical texts, possibly contemporary with the papyri.

28 See Caley 1926.

29 See especially 'Notices sur quelques manuscrits', Berthelot 1888: i 173–219.

Leiden papyrus X offers 101 practical recipes: for making gold and silver, for purifying and assaying metals, for the whitening and bronzing of metals, for attempts to 'increase' metals, for changing the colour of other metals so

ὁ σημαινόμενα τῆς ἐπιστήμης τῶν ἐγκειμένων ἐν τοῖς περὶ χημείας
συγγράμμασι τῶν φιλοσόφων ἣ μάλιστα τῆς μυστικῆς
παραδεδομένης φιλοσοφίας :—

χρυσος                                  ἥλιος χρυσος
χρυσου ρινημα                           σεληνη αργυρος
χρυσου πεταλα                           κρονος φαινον μολιβος
χρυσοι κεκαυμεν                         ζευς φαιθων ηλεκτρος
χρυσηλεκτρον                            αρης πυροεις σιδηρος
χρυσοκολλα                              αφροδιτη φωσφερ χαλκος
μαλαγμα χρυσου                          ερμης στιλβων κασσιτηρος

αργυρος
αργυρου γη
αργυρου ρινημα
αργυρου πεταλα
αργυρο χρυσοκολλα
αργυρος κεκαυμενος                      μολιβδου γη
χαλκος κυπριος                          μολιβδοχαλκος
χαλκου γη                               μολιβδου ρινημα
χαλκου ρινημα                           μολιβδος κεκαυμενος
χαλκου πεταλα                           κασσιτηρος
χαλκος κεκαυμενος                       κασσιτηρου γη
ιοσχαλκου                               κασσιτηρου ρινημα
οριχαλκος                               κασσιτηρου πεταλα
σιδηρος                                 κασσιτηρος κεκαυμενος
σιδηρου γη                              υδραργυρος
σιδηρου ρινημα                          νεφελη
σιδηρου πεταλον                         λευκην παιισαν
σιδηρου ιος                             ξανθην παιισαν
μολιβος                                 λιθαργυρος
                                        θειον απυρον
                                        θειον
                                        θειον αδηκτον
                                        αφρος σεληνον

## SIGNES ALCHIMIQUES DES MÉTAUX

that they will seem gold, writing in gold, and tinting purple. It is taken up with technological processes such as those for alloying gold and silver, working with other metals and making imitation precious stones.[30] In this papyrus there is no alchemical theorization or speculation.

30 Berthelot gives a French translation of this papyrus, 1888: i 28–51.

The contents of the much later Greek manuscripts (as opposed to the papyri) are more varied. They too have recipes and processes, but also letters, allegorical alchemical narratives, accounts of dreams, magical invoca-

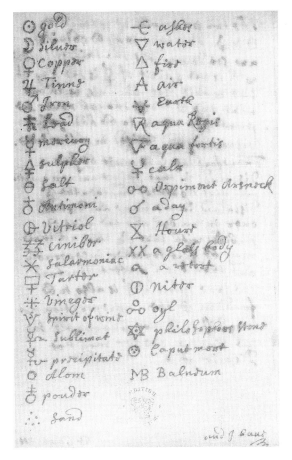

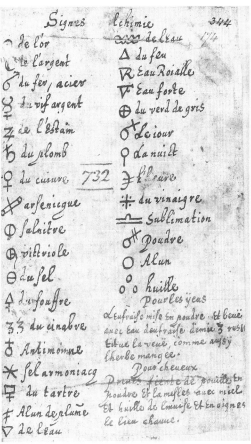

*Fig. 5 (opposite) Symbols for metals and planets from Codex Marcianus Graecus 299, St Mark's Venice. The three lines of Greek across the top read 'The symbols of science of the philosophers found in the technical writings, especially those of the philosophy of them called mystic'. Left-hand column lines 1–7 symbols and kinds of gold; 8–13 symbols and kinds of silver; 14–20 copper; 21–25 iron; 26 lead. The first seven symbols in the right-hand column are of the Sun, Moon, and the planets Saturn, Jupiter, Mars, Venus and Mercury. Codex Marcianus Graecus 299, f.6, from Marcellin Berthelot,* Les origines de l'alchimie *(Paris 1885).*

[BL, 8632.f.14, Planche II, facing p.112.]

*Fig. 6 (above left) Some common alchemical symbols with their meanings.*

[BL, Sloane MS 3772, f.44v.]

*Fig. 7 (above right) 'Signes d'alchimie' from a seventeenth-century collection in French.*

[BL, Sloane MS 732, f.174.]

tions, alchemical poems, and lists of alchemical symbols, substances and synonyms. All these, with the exception of magical invocations, were to be the characteristic contents of later medieval and Renaissance alchemical works.

Some of the language and contents of the later alchemical works are already to be found in these earliest alchemical manuscripts. Zosimos of Panopolis (?c.300AD) is the most important and prolific of the authors in the early manuscripts and the most likely to have been a real person. Already present in some of his writings is the riddling and enigmatic style of so many later alchemical treatises. His works employ enigma and aphorism, including what were to be much-repeated tags: 'Nature overcoming natures' (Nikosa physis tas physeis) and 'a stone but not a stone, a stone unknown and known to all' (lithon ton ou lithon, ton agnoston kai pasi gnoston). Here is a characteristic example of Zosimos's oracular style, from one of several sections 'On the divine water', which may be about mercury*:

> This is the divine and great mystery which is sought. For this is All, and from it the All and through it the All. Two natures, one being, and the one draws the one, and the one has dominance (kratei) over the one. This is mercury [lit: argurion hudor, silver water], the hermaphrodite, which is always escaping, pressing on into its own nature, the divine water of which all have been ignorant, whose nature is hard to contemplate for it is neither metal nor water which is always moving, nor a body, for it is not dominated (krateitai).[31]

31 Berthelot 1888: ii 143–4.

Not only is the preoccupation here with mercury typical of later alchemy, mercury is already characterised, as in later texts, as an hermaphrodite, elusive and fugitive: '*Subtle*: And, what's your mercury? / *Face*: A very fugitive, he will be gone, sir.' Jonson, *The alchemist* [Jonson 1991, II v 31–2]. Zosimos's writings have a typical mixture of chemical process and allegorical vision, the latter already containing motifs standard in later alchemical iconography: the ascent and descent of steps, the dismemberment of a man with a sword and his subsequent transformation (*see* PLATE III), a bubbling vessel, the killing of a dragon.[32] In other early Greek alchemical works there are to be found the analogues for alchemical processes favoured by later alchemical treatises: gold produces gold as wheat does wheat, 'répètent sans cesse les adeptes' as Berthelot says.[33] Later works were regularly to compare the alchemical process to the gestation, birth and nutrition of a child: for 'Cleopatra', in what is probably one of the oldest alchemical texts, philosophers contemplating their alchemical works are like a mother contemplating the fruit of her womb, and the art is like the development of the embryo and then the child.[34]

32 English translations of parts of the visions of Zosimos are given in Taylor 1951: 60–65. These translate Berthelot 1888: ii 107–112, 115–8. *See also* C G Jung, 'The Visions of Zosimos' in *Alchemical studies*, Jung, *Works* 1953–79: xiii 59–108.

33 Berthelot 1885: 51–2.

34 Berthelot 1888: ii 294, iii 282. On the figuring of the alchemical process as generation and birth, *see below*, Chapter 4.

35 Taylor 1951: 46.

In these manuscripts too there are already references to, and descriptions and drawings of, apparatus later developed and used in alchemical operations: the Greek alchemists name about eighty different pieces of apparatus.[35] Zosimos describes the *tribikos*, a three-armed still* (Fig. 11), citing the authority of Mary the Jewess (Fig. 12). Mary the Jewess or Mary the Prophet-

Portavit eum ventus in ventre suo.

Nutrix ejus terra est.

EPIGRAMMA I.

EMbryo ventosâ BOREÆ qui clauditur alvo,
Vivus in hanc lucem si semel ortus erit;
Unus is Heroum cunctos superare labores
Arte, manu, forti corpore, mente, potest.
Ne tibi sit Cæso, nec abortus inutilis ille,
Non Agrippa, bono sydere sed genitus.

B 3                          HER

EPIGRAMMA II.

ROmulus hirtâ lupæ pressisse, sed ubera capræ
Jupiter, & factis fertur, adesse fides:
Quidmirum, teneræ SAPIENTUM viscera PROLIS
Si ferimus TERRAM lacte nutrisse suo?
Parvula si tantas Heroas bestia pavit,
QUANTUS, cui NUTRIX TERREUS ORBIS, erit?

C        Apud

Fig. 8 'The wind carries it in its belly'. The embryo of the Philosophers' Stone can be seen in Boreas's belly. The emblem's motto is part of one of the maxims of the 'Emerald Table'. Michael Maier, Atalanta fugiens (Oppenheim 1617).

[BL, 90.i.19, Emblem I, p.13]

Fig. 9 'Its nurse is the earth', another maxim from the 'Emerald Table'. The earth suckling the infant Philosophers' Stone is flanked by examples of nurture from classical myth: the wolf suckles Romulus and Remus and the goat Amalthea feeds the infant Zeus. Michael Maier, Atalanta fugiens (Oppenheim 1617).

[BL, 90.i.19, Emblem II, p.17]

ess, was sometimes identified with Miriam, the sister of Moses, as in the Jonson quotation from *The alchemist* at the head of this chapter. She was, like Cleopatra, a revered alchemical authority. She is also credited with the invention of the *kerotakis**, probably used for colouring metals, and the particular species of *balneum**, the *bain-marie*, a vessel containing hot water and giving gentle heat, which still bears her name.

Did the writers of these texts think that through their processes they could change other metals into gold and silver? In some recipes there is another precursor of some later alchemical practice, the deliberate intention of fraud. It is possible that in recipes such as those for 'doubling' or 'increasing' gold, that is increasing its weight but decreasing its purity in alloys with other metals, early metallurgists might have thought that they were simply pro-

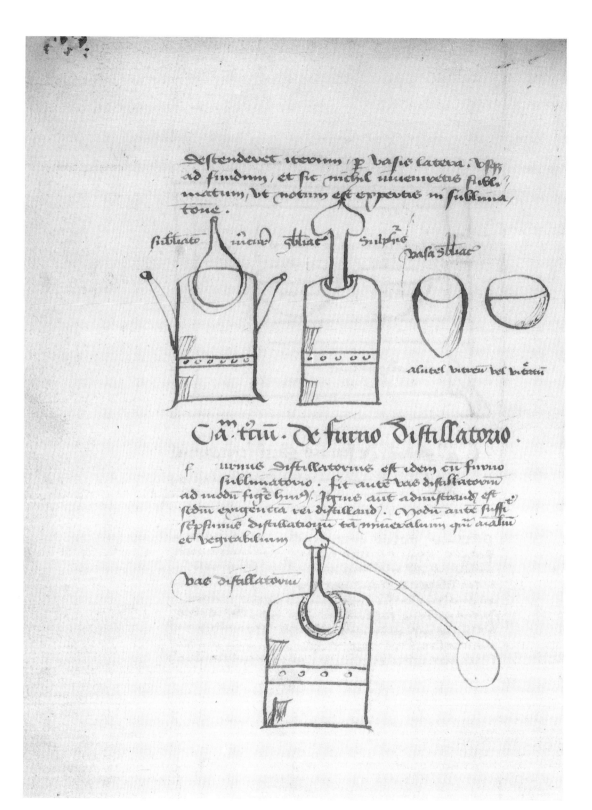

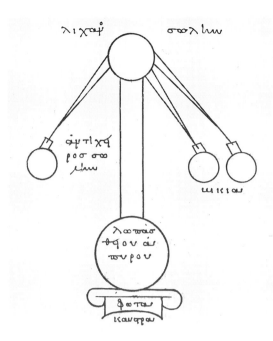

Fig. 10 *(opposite) A fifteenth-century manuscript of* Geber, Liber fornacum: *at the bottom is alchemical apparatus for distillation.*
[BL, Sloane MS 1118, f.61v]

Fig. 11 *(left) The* tribikos. Codex Marcianus Graecus 299, *f.194v, from Marcellin Berthelot,* Collection des anciens alchimistes grecs *(1888).*
[BL, 8906.g.7, i, p.139]

Fig. 12 *(below) Mary the Jewess points to an illustration of her dictum 'Smoke loves smoke': the Latin verses accompanying this engraving announce her as the sister of Moses. Daniel Stolcius,* Viridarium chymicum *(Frankfurt 1624).*
[BL, 717.d.63, figura XVII, sig. F]

36 Berthelot 1888: i 30.

37 On the possible date of the *Turba* and its Greek origins, *see* Plessner 1954.

38 Holmyard 1957: 58–101.

39 The Latin treatises *Liber de septuaginta* ('The book of seventy') and *Liber misercordiae* ('The book of mercy') are exceptions, *see* Halleux 1979: 67. For French translations of these and other works, *see* Berthelot 1893: iii 126ff. On Jabir ibn Hayyan and Geber, *see* Sarton 1927–48: i 532–3 and ii (2) 1043–5, and Holmyard 1957: 66–80.

40 Sarton 1927–48: ii (2) 1043.

41 The manuscripts of all these works of Geber's in The British Library are too numerous to list. BL, Sloane MS 1068 contains them all: 'Gebri Arabi philosophi ... de investigatione perfectionis' ff.133–142; 'Summe perfectionis gebri', ff.143–238; 'Gebri Arabis philosophi ... de Inventione veritatis', ff.239–250; 'Liber fornacum', ff.251–262. Also in The British Library are: *Summa perfectionis*: 'Incipit liber Geber liber perfectionis', BL, Arundel MS 164, ff.131–155, 187–92 (fifteenth century); BL, Sloane MS 1091, ff.3–51 (fifteenth century); BL, Harley MS 3528, ff.43–55v has part of the *Summa perfectionis*. *De investigatione perfectionis*: BL, Sloane MS 1091, ff.75–81 (fifteenth century); BL, Sloane MS 1118, ff.73–80 (fifteenth century); BL, Sloane MS 317, ff.27–30, 'A treattise of Gebare of the investigation or sekinge owt of perfection' (written c.1600). *Liber fornacum*: BL, Sloane MS 1118, ff.60–71 (*see* Fig. 10).

ducing more gold, since they had no fixed ideas about what constituted 'gold'. What did the authors of these processes mean by 'gold'? How much pure gold did it have to contain? On the other hand, a recipe in the Leiden papyrus surely reveals an intention of fraud when it claims to make *asem* (a white alloy resembling silver) 'which will deceive the craftsmen'.[36]

The centre for alchemy in the third century AD was probably Hellenistic Alexandria, as it was also a centre for literature, mathematics, geography, astronomy and philosophy. The contents of these early texts are suggestive of the cultural and philosophic contexts shaping early alchemy: developed technological processes and practical techniques of ancient metallurgy which were originally probably Egyptian; theories of matter and of change from the Greek philosophers, especially Aristotle (*see* Chapter 3, pp.45–50); an animistic belief in a universe instinct with life at all its levels of creation in which entities and events in the heavens were mirrored by those on earth; a mystical cast to religious beliefs, with a belief in spirit intermediaries, magic, astrology, and other esotericisms.

## Arabic alchemy

Alchemical texts reached the Latin west through the medium of Arabic writers. The 'Dark Ages' in Europe were Islamic golden ages of culture and learning which fostered alchemical writings. The names venerated by the early Arabic alchemists were those in the early Greek texts: Democritus, Zosimos, Mary the Jewess and the rest. The technical terms often reveal the transliteration of Greek words into Arabic, e.g. alembic* (al-*ambix*, Greek: the cap of a still). Clearly a text like the Latin *Turba philosophorum* was at some point in its history an Arabic transmission of chemical theory originally Greek.[37]

Of course, to arrive at named authors in Arabic alchemy is only to question the ascription of works to them or even their existence, and we ought perhaps to think rather of pseudo-Geber, pseudo-Rasis and pseudo-Avicenna as the authors of the alchemical treatises. Traditions connected with these Islamic alchemists are recounted by Holmyard.[38]

### Geber

The works of 'Geber', as he was known to the Latin west, may well be doubly pseudonymous. Jabir ibn Hayyan may have flourished about 760AD, although the identity of 'Jabir' is already in doubt in the tenth-century Arabic encyclopaedia *Kitab al-Fihrist* (987AD). Works attributed to him may have been written by his followers in the tenth century, but how much these works represent the thought of Jabir ibn Hayyan must be a matter for conjecture. And many of the Latin treatises ascribed to Geber have no Arabic originals at all,[39] even in the Arabic works from the tenth century. Latin treatises ascribed to Geber began circulating at the close of the thirteenth century and the many manuscripts of 'Geber's' works in The British Library

42 On the *Turba, see* Holmyard 1957: 80–4. For an edition of the Latin text of the *Turba philosophorum* with a German translation, *see Turba,* ed. Ruska 1931; for an English translation *see Turba* tr Waite 1896. BL, Sloane MS 2325, ff.1–6 (fifteenth century) is an extract from the *Turba.* It has annotations by John Dee whose signature is on f.1.

43 On Rasis, *see* Sarton 1927–48: i 609–610 and Holmyard 1957: 84–8.

44 For editions of this work, *see* Steele 1929 and Ruska 1935.

45 BL, Harley MS 3528, ff.76–81v is the *Practica* of Rasis; BL, Harley MS 3703, f.71 'Incipit Practica Rasis' (fourteenth century); BL, Harley MS 3528, ff.164–16 is Rasis, *Lumen luminis* and BL, Sloane MS 1091, ff.85–90 is a fifteenth-century manuscript of the *Lumen luminis.*

46 On Rasis' chemistry, *see* Partington 1938.

47 Ashmole 1652: sig B3.

48 On Avicenna, *see* Sarton 1927–48: i 709–13 and Holmyard 1957: 88–95.

49 Avicenna 1927: 41, 54.

50 *Eg,* a fourteenth-century manuscript of 'Declaratio lapidis per Avicenna filio suo', BL, Harley MS 3703, ff.73v–74v; another manuscript of this treatise is BL, Harley MS 3528, ff.61–62v; a *Tractatulus Avicennae* was printed in *Auriferae artis, quam chemiam vocant* (Basle 1572), 433–67. Some authors who had alchemical treatises ascribed to them seem to have been sceptical or at least wary of alchemy in their genuine works, *eg* Michael Scot and Ramon Lull, *see* Halleux 1979: 101, 107.

testify to their importance and popularity. The *Summa perfectionis magisterii* ('The Summary of the perfection of the magisterium\*') is the most important and famous and was described by Sarton as 'the main chemical textbook of medieval Christendom'.[40] To Geber are also attributed the *Liber fornacum* ('The book of furnaces'), *De investigatione perfectionis* ('On the investigation of perfection'), and *De inventione veritatis* ('On finding out the truth').[41] Geber was an important author for the middle ages. His sulphur–mercury theory of the generation of metals (*see* Chapter 3, pp.50–1) is one of his theoretical contributions derived from Aristotle. He has a preoccupation with the elixir\* (al-*iksir*) or tincture that turns metals to gold and insists on the necessity of carrying out experiments. Four hundred works were attributed to him on magic, astrology, music and philosophy. Latin works of 'Geber', together with another Latin work which was probably translated from Arabic, that collection of sayings attributed to the 'crowd of philosophers,' the *Turba philosophorum* (*see* Chapter 3, Fig. 23),[42] seem to have started circulating at the end of the thirteenth century. They were often cited in and had an enormous influence on alchemical literature of the fourteenth century.

## *Rasis*

Rasis, Rhasis, Rhazes, Razi or al-Razi ('the man of Ray' near Tehran) was the physician, poet and philosopher Abu Bakr Muhammad ibn Zakariyya Al-Razi (*c*.825–*c*.924).[43] Eight alchemical titles are ascribed to him. There was a Latin translation in the twelfth century by Gerard of Cremona of the *Book of secrets*, and *De aluminibus et salibus* ('Concerning alums and salts')[44] and *Lumen luminis* ('The light of light') were said to be his.[45] His works show an interest in the classification and taxonomy of chemical substances and display the range of the laboratory equipment, substances and processes by this time available to the alchemist.[46] With Geber, Arnold of Villanova and the crowned Hermes Trismegistus, 'Rasis' benevolently supervises laboratory operations in Ashmole's *Theatrum* and the fifteenth-century manuscript of Thomas Norton's *Ordinal of alchemy* on which this engraving draws (Fig. 13). Ashmole thought that Rasis was contemporary with Merlin, and even 'his Master in this Abstruse Mystery'.[47]

## *Avicenna*

Avicenna (Abu Ali ibn Sina, 980–*c*.1036)[48] was a physician, philosopher and commentator on Aristotle whose *Canon of medicine* was one of the great medical authorities in the middle ages. In spite of an explicit expression of incredulity about transmutation, in a (pseudo-) Avicennan work (although he allowed that alchemists were good at imitations)[49], Avicenna had alchemical treatises ascribed to him.[50]

Ro: Vaughan. Sculp.

*Fig. 13 (opposite) Alchemical authorities (Hermes, Rasis, Geber, and Arnold of Villanova)*
*overlook alchemical operations in a laboratory. Elias Ashmole,* Theatrum chemicum
Britannicum *(1652). This copy of the* Theatrum *was the author's gift to Thomas Wharton.*
[BL, G.18, 920, p.44]

*Fig. 14 (above) Avicenna points to an emblem of his*
*dictum 'Join together an earthly toad and a flying eagle;*
*you see the magisterium in our art'. Daniel Stolcius,*
Viridarium chymicum *(Frankfurt 1624).*
[BL, 717.d.63, figura XX, sig. F4]

51 Geber's *Summa* and
Avicenna's *De anima*
were among the first
alchemical treatises to be
printed, in Rome 1485
and Paris 1484
respectively, Halleux
1979: 91.

52 On Robert of Chester
and his translation of
this work, *see* Thorndike
1923–58: ii 214–7.

53 Thorndike 1923–58: i
773–4, ii 214–28. It is
typical of alchemical
treatises that the
genuineness of both the
ascription of this
translation and its date
have been questioned.

These three were the Arabic authorities particularly revered by medieval alchemists[51] and it was through such writers that the Latin west was to discover alchemy in the twelfth century, when the words *alkimia, alquimia, alchimia* appear in manuscripts. A twelfth-century manuscript in Berlin begins '*Hic incipit alchamia . . .*' and in 1144 an Englishman writing in Spain, Robert of Chester,[52] declared in the preface to his Latin translation of *The book of Morienus*, 'What alchemy is and what is its composition, your Latin world does not yet know truly'.[53] Through Robert's translation and others like it, the Latin world was almost immediately to learn.

Fig. 15 The title-page of Andreas Libavius, Alchymia, Frankfurt 1606. The words of the title
are flanked by medical and alchemical authorities: Galen on the left, and Aristotle on the right.
Above them are Hippocrates and Hermes, and below them medicine and alchemy are being
practised. Andreas Libavius, Alchymia (Frankfurt 1606).
[BL, 535.k.5, sig. A]

# CHAPTER 2

# ALCHEMISTS AND THEIR WRITINGS

*Subtle:* Who are you?
*Ananias*: A faithful Brother, if it please you.
*Subtle*: What's that?
A Lullianist? A Ripley? *Filius artis*?
Can you sublime, and dulcify? Calcine?

Jonson, The alchemist

Our English Philosophers Generally (like Prophets) have received little honour (unlesse what hath beene privately paid them) in their owne Countrey; . . . But in Parts abroad they have found more noble Reception, and the world greedy of obteyning their Workes; nay (rather then want the sight thereof) contented to view them through a Translation, though never so imperfect. Witnesse what Maierus, Hermannus, Combachius, Faber, and many others have done; the first of which came out of Germanie, to live in England; purposely that he might so understand our English Tongue, as to Translate Norton's Ordinall into Latin verse.

Ashmole, Prolegomena to Theatrum chemicum Britannicum

The end of the twelfth century saw the translation of some Arabic alchemical works into Latin, such as *The book of Morienus* and also the *De aluminibus et salibus* of Rasis. European thought and learning in the thirteenth century was dominated by two Dominicans, Albert the Great and Thomas Aquinas, and a Franciscan, Roger Bacon. All three responded to and assimilated the Aristotelianism that was penetrating the schools, partly through the medium of Arabic commentators on Aristotle. All three mention alchemy in their genuine works and all had alchemical treatises attributed to them.

## The thirteenth century

### Albertus Magnus (c.1200–1280)

The Swabian Dominican, later named *Doctor universalis* by the Roman Catholic church for the breadth of his knowledge, was the dominant figure in learning and the natural sciences in the thirteenth century and its most prolific writer.[1] He was called 'Great' even in his own lifetime. Roger Bacon said Albert was recognised as an authority while still alive, and his pupil Ulric of Strasbourg called him 'the wonder and miracle of our time.' He set himself the formidable task of making Aristotelian knowledge and philosophy, political, logical and scientific, and texts both genuinely Aristotelian

1 For the sources for accounts of Albert's life, *see* Partington 1937.

Fig. 16 Albert the Great points to the alchemical symbol of the hermaphrodite: the motto declares 'All are united in one, which is divided into two parts'. Michael Maier, Symbola aureae mensae *(Frankfurt 1617).*

[BL, 90.i.25, p.238]

2 Thorndike 1923–58: ii 549.

3 *See*, for example, *The book of secrets of Albertus Magnus* ed Michael Best and Frank Brightman (Clarendon Press: Oxford 1973).

4 *Liber mineralium* cited by Thorndike 1923–58: ii 545, 567.

5 Thorndike 1923–58: ii 568.

6 Kibre 1980: 193.

7 Halleux 1979: 102–4; Kibre 1942.

8 Generally on works attributed to Albert and their manuscripts, see Kibre 1942, Kibre 1954, Kibre 1958, Kibre 1959, Kibre 1980.

and some since declared spurious, intelligible to Latin readers. In his lifetime, contemporary with his formidable reputation for learning, legends were already circulating about him as an 'expert in magic', as a contemporary called him.[2] Many spurious treatises located on the borders of the natural and supernatural were subsequently attributed to him: on astronomy, on the wonderful properties of plants and animals,[3] on the secrets of women, and, later still, books of marvels and magic.

Albert's genuine works contain references to alchemy. He went to look at mines and their minerals, and says that he investigated the transmutations of alchemists, and that the art was the one that most closely imitated nature.[4] He accepted the sulphur–mercury theory of the generation of metals (*see* Chapter 3) and seems to have regarded transmutation as possible but difficult; he thought alchemists did not go about it the right way,[5] and never saw transmutation successfully performed.[6] However, he had a reputation as a skilled alchemist shortly after his death and, by the mid-fourteenth century, is mentioned as the author of an alchemical treatise, the *Alkimia minor*. Some thirty alchemical treatises are attributed to him,[7] dating chiefly from the

PLATE III *Alchemical beheading and dismemberment*. Splendor solis.

[BL, Harley MS 3469, f.20v.]

**PLATE IV** *An alchemical compilation from Arnold of Villanova and other authors.*

[BL, Sloane MS 2560, f.1]

PLATE V *The British Library version of the 'Ripley Scroll',*
*1588. This consists of four rolls of various lengths with*
*watercolour drawings. On the second is written 'This long*
*roll was Drawne for me in Cullers at Liubeck in Germany*
*anno 1588'.*

[BL, Additional MS 5025]

PLATE VI *(overleaf)* Thomas Norton, Ordinal of alchemy.

[BL, Additional MS 10,302, f.2]

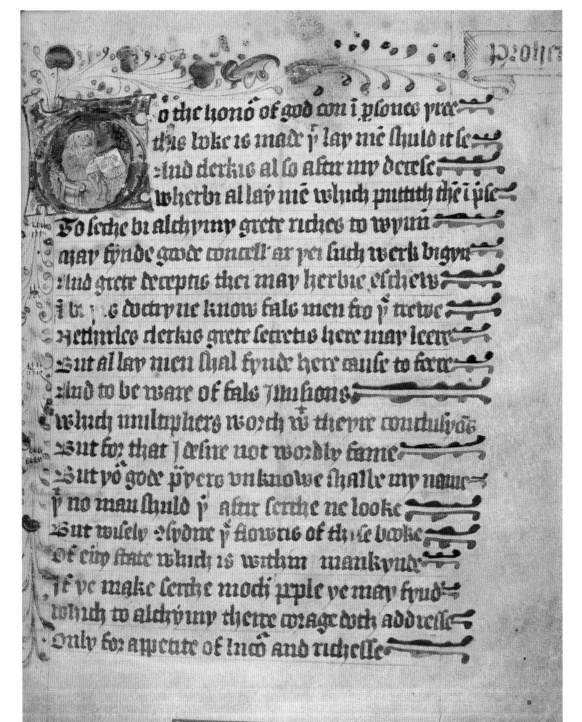

o the honõ of god con i ploueo yere
this boke is made y lay me shuld it se
And clerkis also aftir my devese
wherbi al lay me which puttith thei i ple
To serche bi alchymy grete richies to wynn
may fynde goode councell ar yei such werk bygyn
And grete deceptis thei may herbie eschew
i bi yis doctryne know fals men fro y trewe
Hethirles clerkis grete secretis here may leere
But al lay men shal fynde herr cause to fere
And to be ware of fals Illusions
which multiphers worch w theyre conclusyõs
But for that I desire not worldly fame
But yo gode ppere unknowe shalle my name
y no man shuld y aftir serche ne looke
But wisely aspydne y flowris of these booke
Of eiy state which is within mankynde
If ye make serche moch pple ye may fynd
which to alchymy theyre corage doth addresse
Only for appetite of lucõ and richesse

9 There is a modern English translation, Albertus Magnus 1958.

10 Albertus Magnus 1890–9: xxxvii 545–73.

11 To save cluttering the text with footnotes, details of some manuscripts in the British Library containing works mentioned in this chapter may be found in the appendix. The list does not claim to be complete or exhaustive. For accounts of MSS of Albert's works *see* Kibre 1940, Kibre 1942, Kibre 1944, Kibre 1954, Kibre 1959.

12 Aquinas 1561: III lectio ix, cols 210–13.

13 Aquinas, *Summa* II$^a$ II$^{ae}$, 77, art 2.

14 For an edition and translation *see* Aquinas 1966. There is a very fine 15th century illustrated MS of the *Aurora consurgens*, originally from the monastery at Rheinau and now in the Zentralbibliothek Zurich, Codex Rhenoviensis 172, Aquinas 1966: 26. For illustrations from this manuscript of *Aurora consurgens see* van Lennep 1985: 56–70.

15 Halleux 1979: 104.

16 Halleux 1979: 104–5.

17 There is a MS of this dated 1475 in St Mark's Venice, *see* Thorndike 1923–58: iii 42 fn. 3. It was printed in a collection of alchemical tracts, *Harmoniae inperscrutabilis chymico-philosophiae* (Frankfurt 1625).

18 For accounts of Bacon's life *see* Little 1914: 1–31, Thorndike 1923–58: ii 616–91.

19 *See* Little 1914: 359–72; Molland 1974.

fourteenth and fifteenth centuries.[8] The *Libellus de alchimia*,[9] also known as the *Semita recta* ('The straight path'), is the best-known, and is consistently attributed to him, even being included in the standard edition of Albert's works.[10] The most important of the other treatises ascribed to Albert are the *Alkimia minor*, *De occultis naturae* ('On the secrets of nature'), *De alchimia*, and *Compositum de compositis*. The British Library has manuscripts of the *Semita recta* in Latin, manuscripts containing excerpts in Latin, and also versions of the work in English. It also has manuscripts of the *De occultis naturae*, *De alchimia* and *Compositum de compositis* and other works attributed to Albert.[11]

## Thomas Aquinas (1225/7–1274)

Thomas Aquinas (from Aquino in Italy) came to study with Albert in Cologne in 1244/5. Like Albert, he became a Dominican against parental opposition and preferred a life of scholarship and teaching to career advancements and ecclesiastical high office. Aquinas, in his commentary on Aristotle's *Meteorologica* (378$^{a-b}$)[12] endorsed Aristotle's theory of the generation of metals and knew the theory of the intermediate sulphur–mercury stage ('as the alchemists say', *see* Chapter 3, pp.50–4 below). For him this theory makes the alchemists' generation of metals 'by true alchemical art' just possible now and then – but very difficult, as the influence of heavenly bodies also has a part to play in the formation of metals, an agency very difficult for man to imitate. In the *Summa* Aquinas seems to think that alchemical gold is usually not the same thing as real gold, though again he just allows the possibility that alchemy can also produce the real thing.[13] Aquinas's apocryphal treatise *Aurora consurgens* ('The rising dawn')[14], ('ce texte incompréhensible'[15]) greatly interested Jung. It is a mosaic of quotations from the Bible (particularly from Psalms, Proverbs and above all the Song of Songs) and alchemical authorities such as Avicenna, 'Senior the son of Zadith', Morienus and the *Turba*. Thomas is named by about six alchemical treatises as their author,[16] and a commentary on the *Turba philosophorum* is also ascribed to him.[17]

## Roger Bacon (c.1220–1292)

According to tradition, Bacon was born near Ilchester in Somerset.[18] Whereas Albert is the 'universal doctor', Bacon is the 'wonderful doctor' (*Doctor mirabilis*) who had an even greater reputation than Albert as a magician and wonder-worker in popular literature.[19] Although there are precedents in early romances for such things, there are remarkable passages in *De mirabili potestate artis et naturae* ('On the wonderful power of art and nature') on ships without rowers, flying machines and submarines. Some of these passages found their ways into romances about Bacon. He was described as a necromancer, and was said to have made a speaking brazen head, a tale also told of Albertus Magnus, Robert Grosseteste and Pope Sylvester II. The tradition that he discovered gunpowder is spurious, although he did give directions for making it.

EX SVLPHVRE ET ARGENTO VIVO,
vt natura, sic ars producit me-
talla.

HOMAS AQVINAS ob singularem pieta-
tem & deuotionem *Sanctis* adnumeratus in
doctrinis & scientijs tam admirabilis toti
Christiano orbi apparuit, vt nomen *Angeli-
ci doctoris* adsciuerit, tanquam supra huma-
ni ingenij vim & captum ad spiritualem naturam ascenderet: Qui sane titulus si cui hominum conue-
niat, illi imprimis inuidendus non erit. Tanta enim ille o-
pera quæstionibus subtilissimis & in diuinis & humanis

*Thomas
Angelicus
dictor.*

Zz 3       refer-

*Fig. 17 Thomas Aquinas points approvingly to an illustration of the sulphur–mercury theory:
the natural vapours underneath the earth are imitated in the artificial alchemical process going
on above it. The caption reads 'As nature produces metals from sulphur and mercury, so does
art'. Michael Maier,* Symbola aureae mensae *(Frankfurt 1617).*
[BL, 90.i.25, p.365]

Fig. 18 Roger Bacon. 'Bring the elements into balance and you will have it (ie the Philosophers' Stone)'. Michael Maier, Symbola aureae mensae (Frankfurt 1617).
[BL, 90.i.25, p.450]

20 *See* the account of Bacon in *Biographia Britannica*, 2nd ed, ed Andrew Kippis 1778: i 416–440.

21 Eg Robert Greene's play *Friar Bacon and Friar Bungay* [written c.1589] and *The famous historie of Fryer Bacon* (1627).

Bacon graduated from Oxford, where he 'received the first tincture of letters'[20] and subsequently lectured there and in Paris on Aristotelian and pseudo-Aristotelian works. The tradition that associates him with Brasenose College[21] is ill-founded, as Brasenose was not established until 1509. He entered the Franciscan order, probably in 1257. He was in poor health from c.1256–66, and took little part in university life. In the latter year Pope Clement IV, having heard that Bacon had prepared a major work of learning, and assuming it was already written, repeated a request to see it. Instead Bacon sent him a rapidly completed introduction to the supposed great work, the *Opus majus*, supplemented by the *Opus minor*, and *Opus tertium*. These treatises were in lieu of the great systematic *summa* on all the sciences, including alchemy, he had intended to write. The *Opus majus* criticises the present spirit of science, attempts classification of science and offers an exposition of a new scientific method. Roger anticipated the other Bacon, Francis, in his criticism of the weight of 'authority', his belief in 'experience' and in his plans for a new system and programme of knowledge. For him the most important branches of knowledge included languages, mathematics, optics, 'experimental science' (including alchemy) and moral philosophy.

A work written c.1370 asserts that in 1277 Bacon's teaching was con-

*Fig. 19 Arnald of Villanova gestures to the alchemical marriage of Chabritius and Beia (see Chapter 4, p.89): 'The Stone is obtained from the marriage of Chabricus and Beia'. Maier, Symbola aureae mensae.*
[BL, 90.i.25, p.319]

demned as containing 'suspected novelties' and he was imprisoned until *c.*1291, when he was released. He returned to Oxford where he died in the following year.

In his genuine works Bacon distinguished two sorts of alchemy: speculative (theoretical) and practical, 'which teaches how to make the noble metals, and colours, and many other things better or more abundantly by art than they are made in nature'.[22] Thirty alchemical works are ascribed to Bacon.[23] The best-known are *Tractatus trium verborum* ('The treatise of three words'), *Breve breviarium* ('A short breviary'), *Speculum secretorum alchemiae* ('The mirror of the secrets of alchemy' *Verbum abbreviatum* ('The abridged word'), and the *Speculum alchemiae*. The latter treatise was printed in Latin and French in the sixteenth century and in an English translation which gives this book its name, *The mirror of alchimy*, in 1597. The *Radix mundi* ('The root of the world') which is sometimes ascribed to Bacon, for example in the English translation in William Salmon's *Medicina practica* (1692), is actually by John Sawtre.

22 Quoted by Holmyard 1957: 117.

23 Halleux 1979: 101–2; Singer 1932; Little 1914: 375–426.

# Arnald of Villanova and Ramon Lull

## Arnald of Villanova (c.1240–1311)

Arnald was Catalan and born at Valencia.[24] His early education was in a Dominican convent, and he studied medicine at Naples and at Montpellier, where he also later taught. The majority of his writings are medical. He was a prominent physician, attending to popes (Boniface VIII, Boniface IX and Clement V) and kings (Peter III of Aragon, whom he attended in his last illness in 1285, James II of Aragon and Frederick III of Sicily), sometimes interpreting their dreams for them. The ascription of alchemical writings to Arnald suggests the close association of alchemy and medicine at this period, and alchemy often drew on the theories and discourses of early western medicine. Arnald wrote a book on the distillation* of human blood, recommending as raw material good red blood, extracted in April or May from healthy men between the ages of 25 and 30.[25] The Galenic idea that the ideally healthy and temperate body was constituted by a proper balance of four humours (sanguine, choleric, melancholic and phlegmatic) related to the four elements, was analogous to the Aristotelian theory of the four elements which constituted matter, and the possibility of change between them (*see below*, Chapter 3, pp.45–50). Ill-health occurred when the balance of the humours was upset and good health returned when the physician redressed the balance. In alchemy imperfect metals, often considered as ill, were helped to perfection and an ideal internal balance by the medicine of the elixir. Alchemy teaches 'the restoral (*restituere*) of all fallen and infirm bodies and how to bring them back to a true balance (*temperamentum*) and the best of health'.[26]

Arnald was much travelled and was sometimes employed as a diplomat. He was arrested by the Inquisition in Paris in 1299, but then released. He held critical views of the clergy and Joachite views on the end of the world and the coming of the Antichrist. He died in 1311; an authentic copy of his will survives in the cathedral archives in Valencia.

The alchemical literature attributed to him, a corpus of 57 titles, seems to belong to the fourteenth and fifteenth centuries. The works are easily confused,[27] as some have titles which are used as subtitles for other works by him, *eg Flos florum* ('The flower of flowers') is the title of the treatise with the incipit 'O reverend father I give thanks to God' as well as the subtitle of Arnald's *Perfectum magisterium*. Other titles conceal the fact that they are extracts from longer works, for example, the *Semita semitae* ('The path of the path') is a rearrangement of some chapters from the *Perfectum magisterium*.[28] Thorndike thought some five or six Arnaldian treatises authentic, the others spurious. The tradition that Arnald was an alchemist rests on 'Lullian' texts (*see below* pp.38–41) – his medical treatises seem to indicate that he knew little about alchemy.

Treatises which father themselves upon Arnald have dedications to some of his eminent royal and ecclesiastical patrons and patients: *Questiones tam*

---

24 On Arnald's life and career *see* Thorndike 1923–58: ii 841–61.

25 Thorndike 1923–58: iii 78–80. There is a manuscript of this in Sloane MS 3124 ff. 187v–191, incipit f.187v: 'Incipit epistola magistri arnaldi . . . de separacione elementorum sanguinis humanis'.

26 Lully, *Testament*, quoted in Halleux 1979: 44.

27 An attempt to disentangle them is made by Thorndike, who also lists more minor works, Thorndike 1923–58: iii 654–78.

28 Halleux 1979: 106.

---

*essentiales quam accidentales* ('Enquiries about accidentals as well as essentials') and the *Epistola* to Pope Boniface VIII, to whom Arnald was physician for a year; the *Semita semitae* to Pope Benedict XI; *Epistola ad regem Napolitanum* ('Letter to the king of Naples') to Robert of Anjou, king of Naples; and the *Perfectum magisterium* or *Flos florum* to James II of Aragon.

29 Halleux 1979: 105–7.

The *Rosarius philosophorum* (incipit: *Iste namque liber vocatur Rosarius*), addressed to Cardinal Orsini, is the most famous and also the longest of Arnald's alchemical treatises. The other works are relatively brief and give practical instructions. The *Rosarius* set a fashion for numerous later 'Rosaries' of alchemy,[29] simultaneously proving its popularity, and also increasing the already considerable confusion amongst Arnald's works. It has two parts, theory and practice, a division also popular in later treatises. It exhibits belief in the sulphur–mercury theory, but thinks that mercury is the more important constituent, containing its own internal mercury. It compares the alchemical work to the conception, birth, crucifixion and resurrection of Christ.[30] Chaucer cited Arnald's *Rosarius* in the 'Canon's yeoman's tale': 'Lo, thus seith Arnold of the Newe Toun, / As his Rosarie maketh mencioun', although the passage he refers to, on the dragon and his brother (mercury and sulphur), actually comes in Arnald's *De lapide philosophorum* ('On the philosophers' stone'), not in the better-known *Rosarius*.[31] At any rate, the passage attests the currency that Arnald's works had already achieved in the fourteenth century and the popularity of the *Rosarius* in particular.

30 *See* Holmyard 1957: 122. *See also* Thorndike 1923–58: iii 75–6 and below Chapter 4, pp.79–81.

31 'Canon Yeoman's tale', Chaucer 1957: lines 1428–1447. See also Lowes 1913, Duncan *MLN* 1942.

## Ramon Lull (c.1235–1316)

32 On Lull and the Lullian alchemical corpus *see* Pereira 1989; for a brief account Holmyard 1957: 123–5.

Ramon or Raymund Lull,[32] *Doctor illuminatus* of the Roman Catholic church which placed his works on the Index in the sixteenth century but has since beatified him, was born in Palma, Majorca. A Catalan poet, he wrote love poetry in his youth and also a manual of chivalry which was translated into English by Caxton (?1484). At about the age of 30 he devoted himself to learning and religion and in *c.*1272 experienced a mystical illumination on Mt Randa in which he saw the universe in relation to the *dignitates dei* (dignities of God), divine attributes such as will, virtue, glory, and justice. This illumination informed the Lullian art,[33] a sort of theological taxonomy, based on these divine attributes and designated by letters of the alphabet placed on revolving concentric wheels which then formed new combinations of letters and hence meanings. By analogy, these relationships and categorisations could be extended to other areas: principles, virtues, human faculties, medical concepts. He was an active missionary and hoped to use the logic of his art in converting Muslims. He went three times to North Africa where he is said to have suffered martyrdom by stoning. His will was drawn up in 1313.

33 On the Lullian art and its influence *see* Yates 1954, Yates 1960, Rossi 1961.

*Fig. 20 Ramon Lull. 'The child's body (ie the Philosophers' Stone) comes into motion from the masculine and feminine'. Michael Maier,* Symbola aureae mensae.
*[BL, 90.i.25, p.405]*

## CORPVS INFANTIS EX *MASCVLO* ET
*Fæmina procedit in actum.*

A B *Apenninis Italiæ,* per *Alpes,* *ab Hannibale* per-
vias factas, nec non *Pyræneos,* in *Hispaniam* lõ-
go itinere venimus, vbi *Raymundum Lullium,*
illius gentis (magis nunc ad arma, quam li-
teras promptæ) patronum propter varias.
dotes admirabilem considerabimus: Fuit
hic vir *Protheus* quidam ingenio, *Dædalus* arte, & *Polycletus*
norma iudicii, qui ex maiori *Balearidum insularum* oriundus
in iuuentute liberalibus animum informauit scientiis: Ap-

*Lulius fuit*
*ceu*
*Protheus.*
*Dædalus:*
*Polycletus.*

Stories about Lull, like the formation of the alchemical corpus attributed to him, seem to have gone through successive stages of growth.[34] There was a legend already circulating in the fourteenth century that he was taught the secret of transmutation by Arnald of Villanova and that he in turn disclosed it to Abbot Cremer of Westminster, who had met Lull in Italy and whom he persuaded to return to England with him. There King Edward I, or II, or III, or even 'King Robert' of England persuaded him to make gold, Lull agreeing on condition that the king use it for a pious purpose, such as financing crusades and not fighting fellow Christians. A tradition 'affirmed by an unwritten verity'[35] claimed that the king had rose nobles struck from the metal (they were not minted until 1465) inscribed with *Iesus autum transiens per medium eorum ibat* ('But Jesus passing through the midst of them went his way', Luke 4:30). In a typical alchemical narrative warning against involvement with the great, the king broke his promise, made war on France and imprisoned Lull in the Tower, but eventually Lull 'made himself a Leaper,[36] by which meanes he gained more Liberty' and at length escaped to France.

In works which are genuinely his, Lull seems unfavourable to or even condemns alchemy, and does not believe in transmutation.[37] However, as is the case with Avicenna (*see above* Chapter 1, p.27), this did not prevent the ascription to him of alchemical works, although none is mentioned in lists of Lull's writings drawn up in 1311 and 1314. Lull was not considered an alchemist until the 1370s, well after his death, and is then cited as an alchemical authority from the fourteenth century onwards.[38] There are no manuscripts of 'Lullian' alchemical works before 1500.

There is a large corpus of 143 pseudo-Lullian alchemical works, none of which 'can now be plausibly ascribed to him'.[39] The majority are forgeries written in the late sixteenth century.[40] Pseudo-Lullian alchemical works often imitate genuine Lullian works in their style and in their use of Lullian devices such as figures, diagrams and alphabets. There are lists of alchemical works by Lull in fifteenth-century manuscripts, for example the list of twelve of Lull's works in BL, Sloane MS 75 f.185v. This catalogues the following important alchemical works: *Testamentum*, *Codicillus*, *Apertorium*, *Quaestiones* and *Tractatus ad regem Robertum*. The *Testamentum*, which set the fashion for later alchemical wills and testaments,[41] claims to have been composed in England and is the oldest and most important work attributed to Lull. It is really a cluster of treatises,[42] in manuscripts often divided into four parts: *Theorica*, *Practica*, *Liber mercuriorum* ('The book of mercuries'), and *Practica de furnis* ('A practical treatise about furnaces'), and was followed by the *Cantilena*. The work employs letters and figures in the same way as the genuine Lullian *ars*. A number of summaries of, and commentaries on, the *Testamentum* soon appeared, in which English alchemists were particularly interested. There was an initial transmission of pseudo-Lullian alchemy to England in the early fifteenth century and its doctrines were popularized by Ripley (*see below* p.41) in the 1470s. The *Codicillus* describes the stages of the alchemical operation as being like the generation of the

34 See Pereira 1989: 38–49.

35 Ashmole 1652: 443.

36 Ashmole 1652: 467; 'leper' seems to me the most likely gloss and explanation here.

37 Thorndike 1923–58: ii 867 and iv 4–8.

38 Thorndike 1923–58: ii 862–73.

39 Pereira 1989: 1. On the pseudo-Lullian alchemical corpus *see* Pereira 1989, Halleux 1979: 107–9 and Thorndike 1923–58: iv 3–64. For very fine illuminations from a manuscript of Lull's *Opera chemica* in Florence [Bibliotheca Nazionale Centrale MS BR 52] *see* van Lennep 1985: 79–84.

40 For extensive catalogues of works attributed to Lull and their manuscripts *see* Pereira 1989: 61–107 and Thorndike 1923–58: iv 619–52.

41 Cf Basilius Valentinus, *Fratris Basilii Valentini ... Geheime Bücher oder letztes Testament* Strassburg 1645 and the English translation *Basilius Valentinus ... His last will and testament* London 1657.

42 *See* Singer 1928.

human body (*see below*, Chapter 4, pp.82–9). The *Liber de secretis naturae seu de quinta essentia* ('The book of nature's secrets, or Concerning the fifth essence') was written at the beginning of the fifteenth century. Confusingly, some works in the corpus are often commentaries, abbreviations, or supplements to others in the corpus.

## Fifteenth- and sixteenth-century English alchemists

### George Ripley (early fifteenth century–c.1490)

George Ripley[43] was born in the early fifteenth century in the village of Ripley near Harrogate and died *c.*1490. He studied alchemy and other subjects at Rome, Louvain and on Rhodes, where he supposedly made gold for the Knights of St John, giving them £100,000 a year. In 1471 he was a canon of an Augustinian Priory at Bridlington where the fumes of his laboratory annoyed the rest of the community. He popularized the teachings of Lull, with whose writings his have great affinity, as Ashmole noted.[44] He also wrote a *Cantilena* in imitation of Lull's,[45] which has the subtitle *De lapide philosophorum, seu de phenice* ('On the philosophers' stone, or On the phoenix'; *see* Chapter 4, PLATE XVII). His *Compound of alchemy* was dedicated to Edward IV and was written in English. It was one of the earliest alchemical texts to be printed in England, in 1591 (*Compound of alchymy*, BL C.39.d.26). His *Concordantia Guidonis et Raimundi* ('Bringing into agreement Guido and Raymund [Lull]' probably appeared after 1471. There are numerous manuscripts of the *Medulla alchemiae* ('The marrow of alchemy') which in 1476 he dedicated to George Nevill, archbishop of York. He was said to have been the instructor of Thomas Norton. An edition of his works was printed in Latin, in Cassel, 1649.

### Thomas Norton (?1433–1513/4)

Thomas Norton[46] came from a well-known Bristol family: his grandfather had been the town's mayor. His great-grandson Samuel tells us that his ancestor was a member of Edward IV's privy chamber. Samuel continued his family's alchemical tradition in the next century and wrote *The key of alchimie* in 1577. In 1479, Thomas Norton accused the mayor of Bristol of treason, and in the course of settling the dispute some details of his life emerge. Norton was described as haunting taverns, neglecting divine service and playing tennis on Sunday afternoons. He came out of this dispute badly and charges against the mayor were dismissed.

Norton was said to have corresponded with Ripley, who agreed to make him 'heire unto this Arte'; he studied with Ripley for forty days when he was 28. He is supposed to have twice succeeded in making the elixir of life, only to have it stolen from him, once by a servant and once by a Bristol merchant's wife. His alchemical fame rests on his *Ordinal of alchemy* which was given pride of place in Ashmole's *Theatrum* (1652). A Latin translation by Michael Maier had been printed in 1618 in Frankfurt, in Maier's *Tripus aureus* ('The

43 On Ripley *see* Holmyard 1957: 182–5.

44 Ashmole 1652: 458.

45 For an edition of the English text *see* Taylor, 'George Ripley's song' 1946.

46 For a full account of what is known about Norton's life see Norton 1975: xxxvii–lii, Reidy 1957, and also Holmyard 1957: 185–95.

golden tripod'). There seems no reason to doubt Norton's assertion that the *Ordinal* was begun in 1477, and equally there is now no reason to doubt his authorship,[47] which the poem conceals in a cypher. There are nine manuscripts of this work in The British Library, including a late fifteenth-century illuminated work (*see* PLATES II, VI and XIII), very similar to, but not identical with, the copy on vellum which Ashmole describes a gentleman lending him.[48] There is no evidence of the other works that Ashmole mentions having been attributed to Norton, the *De transmutatione metallorum* and *De lapide philosophorum*.

47 Doubts expressed in Nierenstein 1932 and Nierenstein 1934 were convincingly dispelled in Reidy 1957 and by Reidy again, Norton 1975.

48 Ashmole 1652: 455.

### Thomas Charnock (1526–81)

49 On Charnock *see* Holmyard 1957: 195–200, Taylor 1946.

Thomas Charnock[49] was born in Faversham, Kent in 1526. He travelled all over England in search of alchemical knowledge and became friendly with one 'J S' who bequeathed him the alchemical secret on his death in 1554. However, on New Year's Day, 1555, Charnock's apparatus was destroyed when the wooden casing of his alchemical vessel caught fire, and he was forced to learn the secret again from Holway, Prior of Bath. He again spent several months at work, but just as success was near he was conscripted for military service against the French at Calais in 1557. In rage he smashed his apparatus to pieces with a hatchet. In 1562 he married Agnes Norden of Stockland Bristol in Somerset, and moved to Combwich near Bridgewater where he set up a laboratory and pursued his experiments, finally achieving success in 1574. He died in 1581. He wrote 'A book of philosophie', which he dedicated to Elizabeth I and of which he delivered a copy to Lord Burghley. His *Breviary of naturall philosophy*, begun 1 January 1557 and finished in July of the same year is included in Ashmole's *Theatrum chemicum Britannicum*, together with two 'Aenigmas' and some fragments.

*Fig. 21 From left to right, Basil Valentine, Abbot Cremer and Thomas Norton in conversation in an alchemical laboratory. Michael Maier,* Tripus aureus, *(Frankfurt 1618).*
*[BL, 1033.k.7 (2), title-page]*

# TRIPVS AVREVS,

Hoc est,

# TRES TRACTATVS

## CHYMICI SELECTISSIMI,

*Nempe*

I. BASILII VALENTINI, BENEDICTINI ORDI-
nis monachi, Germani, PRACTICA vna cum 12. clauibus &
appendice, ex Germanico;

II. THOMÆ NORTONI, ANGLI PHILOSOPHI
CREDE MIHI seu ORDINALE, ante annos 140. ab authore scriptum, nunc ex Anglicano manuscripto in Latinum
translatum, phrasi cuiusque authoris vt, & sententia retenta;

III. CREMERI CVIVSDAM ABBATIS WEST-
monasteriensis Angli Testamentum, hactenus nondum publi-
catum, nunc in diuersarum nationum gratiam editi, & figuris
cupro affabre incisis ornati operâ & studio

*MICHAELIS MAIERI* Phil. & Med. D. Com. P. &c.

FRANCOFVRTI
Ex Chalcographia Pauli Iacobi, impensis LVCÆ IENNIS.
Anno M.DC.XVIII.

*Fig. 22 The middle of the alchemical work: Conjunction. The steps ascending up the alchemical mount are calcination, sublimation, solution, putrefaction, distillation, coagulation and then tincture. Steffan Michelspacher,* Cabala: Spiegel der Kunst und Natur in Alchymia *(Augsburg 1616).*

[BL, 1032.c.3, (1), Plate III]

ALCHEMICAL THEORIES AND PRACTICES

# CHAPTER 3

# ALCHEMICAL THEORIES AND PRACTICES

... though the Philosophers speak plurally
All is but one thing you may me well trowe.

Ripley, 'Epistle to King Edward IV', Compound of alchymy

What else are all your terms,
Whereon no one o' your writers 'grees with other?

Jonson, The alchemist

This operation is indeed a Labyrinth.

Nicholas Flamel, Nicholas Flamel, his exposition of the Hieroglyphicall figures

... in a sustained course of reading, each tract in this illimitable ocean of alchemical literature heightens the general impression of an irremediable confusion of expression, thought, and method.

John Read, Prelude to chemistry

Greek philosophers before Plato and Aristotle, particularly the Sicilian Empedocles (492–432BC), had theories about the nature of matter, the elements which made it up, and how one could change into another. The idea of four elements, fire, air, water and earth, as the basis of matter was therefore already in place in Plato's *Timaeus* (written *c*.360BC), which has a claim to be the first treatise on theoretical chemistry and was the only dialogue of Plato's which was known to Europe before the late twelfth century. However, it is Aristotle's theories about matter which were more significant for later alchemy.

According to Aristotle, an element is an irreducible constituent of material things, actually or potentially present in them and into which they can be divided (*diaireitai*).[1] There are four fundamental properties: hot, moist, cold and dry; and four elements: fire, water, air and earth. All bodies are composed of these elements in different proportions and combinations. It follows that to change the proportion and combination of these elements in a body would be to make a different body. The elemental principles are not to be thought of as actual flames or drops of water and so on, although the former would be present in the latter, and they are constituted by pairs of defining qualities:

1 Aristotle, *De caelo* 302a.

## Propositio XIII.
### & ultima.

Id tantùm quod compositum est
ex oleo incombustibili, & de sale fu-
sibili, est amicabile huic arti. Ex hoc
maximè elicitur, quòd lapis Physicus
componitur ex oleo incom-
bustibili, & sale fuf-
sibili.

*Deo gratias, amen.*

| | |
|---|---|
| *Fire:* | hot and dry |
| *Air:* | hot and moist |
| *Water:* | cold and moist |
| *Earth:* | cold and dry |

Although the elements are constituted by these pairs of contrary qualities (fire, being hot and dry, is the opposite to water, which is cold and moist), they may change into one another, as Aristotle stated, 'We maintain that fire, air, water and earth are transformable one into another, and that each is potentially latent in the others'.[2] Changes between elements is easier when

2 Aristotle, *Meteorologica* 339b.

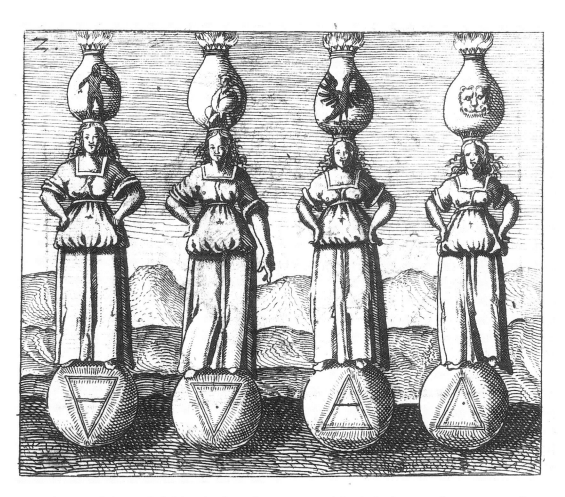

Fig. 23 (opposite) ('The crowd of philosophers', Auriferae artis . . . sive Turba philosophorum, *Basle 1572.*

*[BL, 717.e.38, sig.)( 8v]*

Fig. 24 (above) The elements as four women, standing on globes engraved with the elements' common alchemical symbols. They are arranged from left to right in order of ascending subtlety: earth, water, air and fire. Herbrandt Jamstahler, Viatorium spagyricum *(Frankfurt 1625).*

*[BL, 1034.k.2, (1), p. 76]*

they share a common characteristic; as in the case of fire and air which are both hot, and air and water, which are both moist. Between others it is slower and more difficult, as these elements do not have qualities in common, as is the case with fire and water. Change between the elements was imagined to go around in a circle[3] (*see* figs 25 and 26). Alchemical treatises were later habitually to think of change as change of and among the four elements: 'turn earth into water, then into fire, and fire into air, and hide the fire in the inmost parts (*in intimis*) of the water'.[4] An anonymous English alchemical poem in Elias Ashmole's *Theatrum chemicum* (1652) put all these theories – the four elements, their pairs of characteristics and shared characteristics, and their circular change one into another – into (not very good) verse:

3 Aristotle, *De generatione et corruptione* 328a–332a.

4 *Turba philosophorum* in *Auriferae artis* 1572: 125.

Fig. 25 *The elements from a 15th century MS of Artephius,* Clavis sapientiae, *Additional MS 10,764 ff. 117–126v.*
*f.120: the elements go around in 'the philosphers' wheel', in which adjacent elements share one characteristic in common.*
*f.121: the top diagram shows the four elements, the lower diagram the four qualities:* frigiditas *(cold),* humiditas *(moisture),* siccitas *(dryness) and* caliditas *(heat).*
[BL, Additional MS 10764, ff.120 and 121]

Putrefacio ⸭ phorum

Nigredo
et lucida

tram partes
ini tm

Aqua

~ Caput ~                    Coruu ~

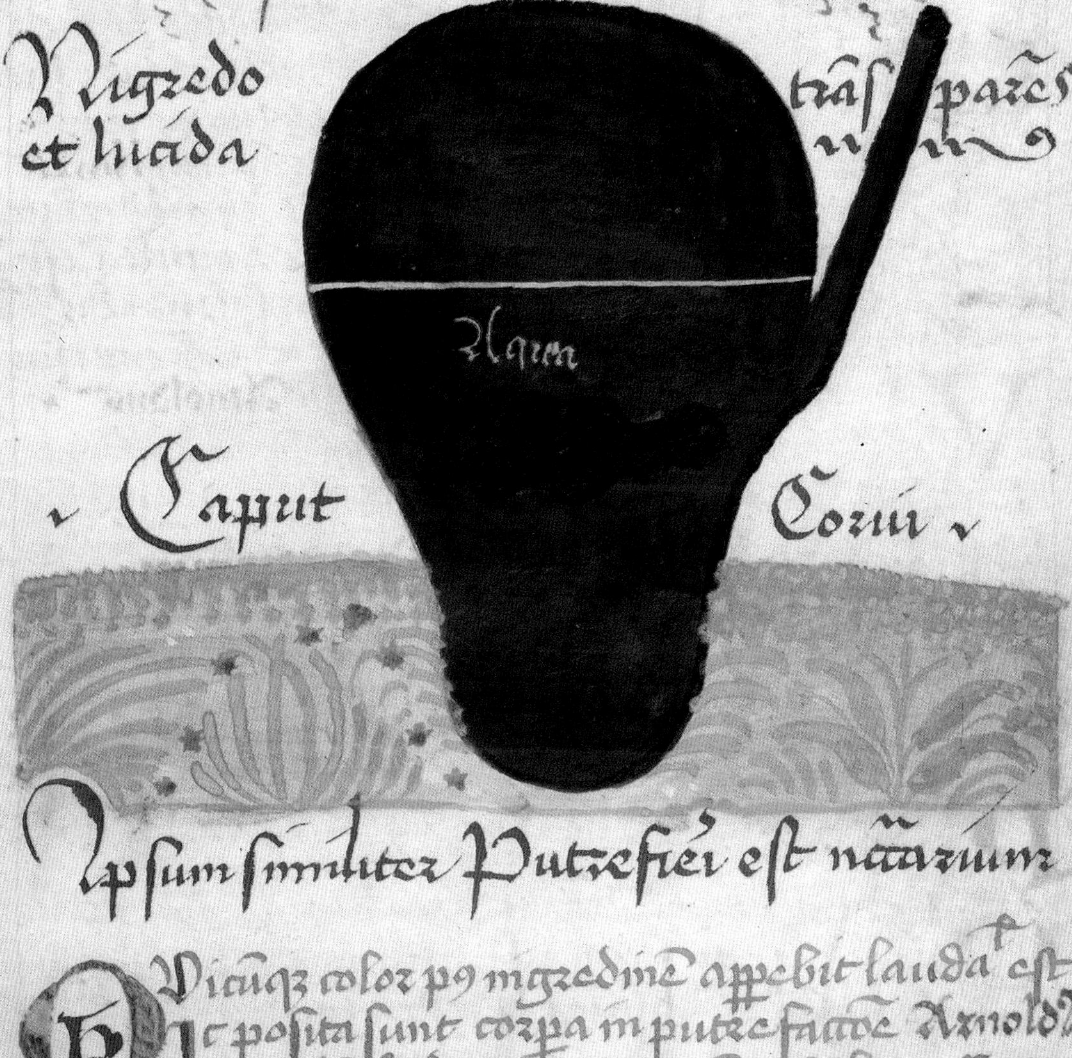

Ipsum similiter Putrefieri est nĩctarium

Vicuqʒ color pg nigredine apebit lauda⁴ est
Hic posita sunt corpa m putrefacõe Arnold⁹
et efficiut⁹ tra nigra Et tu videbis māx de
nigrari · Gaude · quia prĩcipiu est digestiõis
Coburce iᵈ es nrm igne levi sic Arnoldus
Conor nutrip donet corpꝫ eiuꝫ ostituat⁹ et
tinctura extrahat⁹ Non aut extrahas eã tota si
mul Sʒ par et par egrediat⁹ omni die donet in
longp opleant tempe Hermeꝫ pater phorum

Gosum māx albi et rubeus albi et ãtinuꝫ

PLATE VIII *The green lion devouring the sun from 'The Booke of the Rosary of philosophers', written in Lübeck 1588. The captions reads 'Of our Mercury which is the grene Lyon devowringe the Sonne'.*
[BL, Additional MS 29,895, f.119v]


*Fig. 26 (opposite) The* catena aurea *(golden chain) of the elements, showing the 'links' between them.*
[BL, Sloane MS 2476, f.10v]

Qudam vero fatui non intendentes nec intelligentes verba enigma-
tica philosophorum ac eorum contradictiones minime inspicientes et sibi
industriam naturalem non consequentes non inquirentes nec scientes
naturam metallorum hanc artem sepius inceperunt et de fine lauda-
bili nequaquam assequuntur verius autem testamentum dicit Quapropter
est multorum sed finis autem paucorum Nam vera infallibilis
inceptio est unde sit quodammodo metallum quod omni in prima generatione
naturo quid in ministerio manuum humanorum et quid in finis tem-
porum quia si fundamentum huius operis sit inceptum in natura ab opere
non dimittit bono prolixitatis regimine quousque perficiat Quoniam quod
natura dedit nemo tollere potest Et alibi ex aliorum auctoritate philosophorum
ubi a natura dimittitur ab opere incipitur.

Signum sublimis generans:

Aer qui est calidus et humidus

Catheua

Spiritus quinte essentie to-
tum illud perficit et magist-
rium supra in fine totius
operis ad complementum si eum
artifex sit ingeniosus et non
nimis festinus nec in opere
capitosus sed de bono proposito
eadem arte uti illa et postea
secrete custodia et vendo
precium impotente pretium conse-
dato et ei mandata fiat custodia.

Aurea

Terra que est frigida et sicca

Signus naturalis agens

First Fire in Nature is hott and dry,
Aire differs from Fire in moisture only:
Earth only for coldnesse from Fire disagrees,
This Concord and discord every man sees:
Aire hot and moist of complexion and kinde,
Water differs from Aire but in heate we finde:
Soe that in moysture we finde them both one;
Naturall heate in Water we finde none;
Water cold and moiste of Complexion is,
Earth differs from Water in drynes I wis:
Earth agrees with Fire in drynes noe doubte,
Thus one in another the Wheele turnes about.[5]

5 Ashmole 1652: 404–5.

A similar principle applies in the case of actual material things, as opposed to their constituent elements; some things are contraries and cannot be changed directly into one another, for example a dead thing cannot change directly into a living thing. In these cases the thing must first return to matter (*hyle*) before change into its opposite can take place.[6]

6 Aristotle, *Metaphysics* 1044b.

In the air immediately surrounding the earth, said Aristotle, the vapour is naturally moist and cold and contains exhalations from the earth that are hot and dry. Many phenomena, for example apparitions of burning flames in the sky, are the result of an 'exhalation' (*anathumiasis*) or rather a combination of two exhalations, one vaporous and rising from water, the other drier, rising from the earth and more like wind or smoke.[7] Similarly, says Aristotle in a passage at the end of *Meteorologica* book III, which was seminal for later alchemical theory, these 'exhalations' or 'secretions' (*ekkrisis*) also occur below ground, and there they are the origins of minerals. The dry, earthy, hot, smoky exhalations produce 'diggable things' (*okurta*), that is, stony, dusty minerals, the vaporous exhalation produces metals (*metalleuetai*) which can be melted and which are workable, such as iron, gold and copper. In the case of metals, this moist exhalation is enclosed, especially within stones, where it is compacted by drier surroundings and its moistness solidifies.

7 Aristotle, *Meteorologica* 340b–341b.

To sum up, minerals are produced by a moist or dry exhalation, or by the interaction of the two, as in the case of metals when the moist exhalation is compressed by the dryness of stones. Metals 'are in a sense water (*dio esti men os hudor tauta*)' but are solidified before the exhalation is turned to water. In addition, all metals are affected by fire, with the exception of gold, and also contain earth.[8]

8 Aristotle, *Meteorologica* 378a–b.
9 Avicenna 1927.

'Geber' (*ie* pseudo-Jabir ibn Hayyan) and later pseudo-Avicenna[9] followed Aristotle's account of the generation of metals but postulated an intermediate stage, the formation in the earth by Aristotle's moist and dry exhalations of, respectively, 'mercury' and 'sulphur', which then combine in various degrees and proportions to form the metals. Just as Aristotle's 'fire' and 'water' were elemental principles, so Geber's 'sulphur' and 'mercury' are alchemical *principles*, or internal and constitutive rudiments, not the common minerals. By the thirteenth century this theory seems common-

50                                    ALCHEMICAL THEORIES AND PRACTICES

10 Thorndike 1923–58: ii
471–2.

11 Bacon, *Speculum
alchemiae* quoted Read
1939: 24.

12 Paracelsus, *De natura
rerum* bk I quoted
Crosland 1962: 14.

13 George Ripley, 'The
mistery of alchymists' in
Ashmole 1652: 382;
Norton 1975: lines
2397–8.

14 Geber, *Summa*, Geber
1991: 278.

15 Aristotle, *De caelo*
271a and 288.

16 Thorndike 1923–58: ii
447.

17 Geber, *De
investigatione perfectionis*
in Geber 1545: 2.
18 Geber 1991: 471.

19 Geber 1991: 489.

20 Geber 1991: 507–8.

place. Vincent of Beauvais refers to the generation of metals from sulphur and mercury in the bowels of the earth,[10] and Thomas Aquinas lent authority to this idea (*see above*, Chapter 2, p.33, and Fig. 17). Medieval works, for example, pseudo-Bacon's *Speculum alchemiae*,[11] abound in this theory, which was to survive until the end of the seventeenth century. A third principle, that of salt, was later added, and the theory of the *tria prima* (three first principles) was held by Paracelsus, and others. An analogy was drawn between mercury, sulphur, and salt composing the nature of metals and (respectively) spirit, soul and body composing the nature of man: 'Mercury is the spirit, sulphur is the soul and salt is the body'.[12] Mercury and sulphur were indwelling in metals, and spirit and soul in the body, as fishes in the sea or animals in a wood.

Similarly, the alchemical medicine that would transform metals was said to be composed of *corpus*, *spiritus* and *anima*.[13] It was not until the late seventeenth century that voices were heard, like that of Robert Boyle in *The sceptical chymist* (1661), expressing doubt about Aristotle's four elements and the metallic principles:

> The Experiments wont to be brought, whether by the common Peripateticks, or by the vulgar Chymists, to demonstrate that all mixt bodies are made up precisely either of the four Elements, or the three Hypostatical Principles, do not evince what they are alledg'd to prove ...

But the sulphur–mercury theory prevailed for most of alchemy's lifetime and provided the premise on which the theory of transmutation rested. Nature, says Geber, bases her activities on mercury and sulphur.[14] Now Aristotle had observed, 'Nature does nothing in vain, but aims at final causes' and 'Nature and God are working towards an end, striving for what is perfect',[15] and Roger Bacon was to agree: 'Nature has always had for an end and tries ceaselessly to reach perfection, that is gold'. Bacon's older contemporary, Robert Grosseteste, said all metals should be gold, but varied in their degrees of imperfection.[16] Geber said that the cause of perfection in metals in nature (that is, gold and silver) is a properly proportionate mixture of mercury and sulphur and long and temperate maturing by heat (*decoctionem*) in the bowels of the earth, where the mixture is eventually rendered fusible and malleable. Conversely, lack of perfection (that is, in tin, lead, copper and iron) is caused by lack of proportion and purity and insufficient proper heat.[17] Gold is made from a combination of the most subtle, fixed and brightest mercury with a little clear, fixed, red sulphur.[18] Silver is made from a combination of mercury and white sulphur, and the other metals from varying and less stable mixtures of mercury and sulphur, in less pure forms. Geber says at various points that the greater the proportion of mercury in a body, the greater its perfection,[19] and as a result of these various combinations, copper is comparatively the most perfectible of metals and lead the least.[20] Since all metallic bodies are composed of mercury and sulphur, imperfect bodies can be changed by taking away superfluity and impurity and supplying deficiency.

*93*

Nvn ist von nöthen daß ihr wißt/
Im Wald ein Hirsch vnd Einhorn ist.

Die dritte Figur.

In Corpore est Animâ & Spiritus.

M iij                                    Die

The development of this alchemical theory from Aristotle's premises onwards is neatly summarized in the argument with which the alchemist Subtle tries to persuade the sceptical Surly in Ben Jonson's *The alchemist* (first performed in 1610). Subtle's by-now standard alchemical arguments – that the prime matter of metals is humid exhalation enclosed in crass earth, that mercury and sulphur 'are the parents of all other metals', that lead and other metals would be gold if they had time, and that alchemy helps that process along – were taken as found by Jonson in a discussion of alchemy in a late sixteenth-century book on magic by the Jesuit Martin Del Rio.[21] Surly's voice was not the only one in the early seventeenth century sceptical about the progressive theory of metals 'growing up'. Though Francis Bacon, like Aquinas, allowed that, theoretically, making gold might be possible, he was sceptical of the theory of metals 'growing up' into the perfection of gold,

21 *See* Jonson, *Works* 1925–52: x 81–82.

*Fig. 27 (opposite) The deer and unicorn are in the wood as 'Soul and Spirit are in the body'.* Von Lambsprinck, Lambspring: das ist Ein herlicher Tractat vom Philosophischen Steine *in Hermanus Condeesyanus (ie Joannes Grassenus),* Dyas chemica tripartita *(Frankfurt 1625).*

[BL, 1034.h.21, p. 93]

*Fig. 28 Following Nature's footsteps. 'May Nature, reason, experience and books be guide, staff, spectacles and lamp for the chemical practitioner'. Michael Maier,* Atalanta fugiens *(Oppenheim 1617).*

[BL, 90.i.19, Emblem XLII, p. 177]

22 Francis Bacon 1627:
86.

... that Nature hath an intention to make all metals gold, and that if she were
delivered from impediments, she would performe her owne worke ... all these
are but dreames ...[22]

23 Petrus Bonus 1546:
f. 20, f. 77.

24 Thorndike 1923–58: ii
567.

Alchemy could claim to follow nature, but to speed up its process of perfecting metals. The alchemical art was minister to and follower of nature,[23]
indeed Albertus Magnus (in a genuine work) said that it was the art that most
closely imitated nature;[24] starting with the same first principles of 'our mercury' and 'our sulphur', imitating nature's heat – in the alchemical furnace –
and nature's enclosed, dryly compacting space beneath the earth where gold
is formed – in the sealed alchemical vessel. But whereas nature took thou-
sands of years gradually to generate gold and silver from mercury and sul-

25 Rasis, Steele 1929: 27.

phur, God could bring this about in a day,[25] and so, said later authorities,
could the alchemical art in which the operators were nature's helpers or
ministers.

Geber thought that bodies could be brought back to perfection in two
ways: preparation followed by the commixture of imperfect with perfect

26 Geber, Liber fornacum
in Geber 1545: 198ff.

bodies, or by the medicine.[26] The first idea, that of the fermentation* of gold,
by leavening less perfect metals with the perfect, persisted for some time. It
probably had its origins in Greek texts where the inclusion of gold or silver
in alloys was thought of as a seed or ferment which would cause the whole
alloy to become precious metal. Albertus Magnus gives fermentum as the
Latin gloss for the Arabic elixir and says that 'just as bread is leavened and

27 Albertus Magnus, De
alchimia in Gratarolus
1561: 84.

raised through good yeast, so is the matter of metals transmuted'.[27] However,
the idea of a powerfully curative medicine or transforming elixir became
more dominant than that of gold as a seed or ferment, although both ideas of
the elixir, as medicine and ferment, are still present in Martin Rulandus'

28 Rulandus 1612:
197–8.

definition of the elixir in his alchemical Lexicon (1612).[28] Bacon says that
alchemy is a science teaching the transformation of metals and this transfor-

29 Bacon, Speculum
alchimiae in Geber 1541:
258.

mation is effected by a medicine (medicinam propriam).[29] One difference
between the idea of a ferment and the tincture* effected by the medicine
seems to have been that the medicine was thought to transmute instantly, 'by a

30 Rulandus 1612: 384.

sudden entry (repentino ingressu)'[30] in the moment of projection*, as opposed
to the slower process implied in ferment. Geber describes three grades of
medicines in ascending order of efficacy: effecting some change on imperfect
bodies, effecting a change resulting in one of the characteristics of perfection,

31 Geber 1991: 546–8.

effecting a change that achieves perfection.[31] As Arnold of Villanova
declared,

> There abides in nature a certain pure matter, which being discovered and
> brought by art to perfection, converts to itself proportionally all imperfect
> bodies that it touches.

32 An idea repeated in
the section on alchemy
in John Gower, Confessio
amantis, printed in
Ashmole 1652: 370–1.

Some thought that there were actually three stones, animal, vegetable and
mineral,[32] with the respective properties of curing, stimulating growth and
transmuting metals; however, the consensus was that there was only one
Stone, just as the treatises are fond of proclaiming the unity and simplicity of
alchemy.

Despite the repeated claim of alchemical treatises that really all the philosophers and authorities spoke with one voice, there was no unanimity about the successive alchemical processes that eventually produced this elixir or medicine, merely a tradition of how one might tell if the process was going well. There was some agreement from about the fifteenth century onwards that the processes were signalled by the colours black, white (shining like the eyes of fishes said later alchemists[33]) and finally a deep red appearing in the glass vessel in which the Stone was made, and in that order: 'Rede is last in werke of alchymye',[34] and Solomon Trismosin described the final stage as a red so beautiful that no scarlet could compare with it[35] (*see* PLATES VII, X and XI). Colours appearing out of this order, such as the too early appearance of red, or a later return of the black stage, signalled failure, although some writers said that all the colours were repeated during multiplication* of the Elixir,[36] multiplication being a reiteration of an earlier part of the work,[37] or even occurring just before the red stage. These colours were described in the early Greek texts, which also included a yellow stage (*xanthosis*, 'yellowing') between the white and the purple stage (*iosis*, 'refinement, making of tincture').[38] These four colours are those listed by Pliny as used by ancient artists in painting. The distinction between the yellow stage, which was the making of gold, and the final purple stage is not entirely clear in the early Greek texts, and might go some way to explaining the ambiguity in some later alchemical works about a final red *or* citrine stage, or a citrine stage just preceding the final red stage, 'Yellow the messenger of the Redd'.[39] Some confusion may have arisen as a result of translation. For example, the 1591 English translation of Bacon's *Speculum alchimiae* says ambiguously that 'the red Elixir doth turne into a citrine colour infinitely' whereas the Latin text seems to claim that the red elixir colours other things yellow (that is, possibly, makes them gold).[40] Paracelsus listed the colours as black, white, citrine and red.[41] But there were further variations on this basic theme of black-white-red. The treatise *Splendor solis* quotes the Philosopher Miraldus' claims in the *Turba philosophorum* that the Stone turns black, yellow and red twice,[42] while in the *Turba* the philosopher Zenon says that the Stone is black and citrine on the first day of its composition, black and red on the second, citrine on the third and finally purple.[43] George Ripley, in a stanza from the 'Recapitulation' of his *Compound of alchymy*, lists the succession of true and false colours, described figuratively and including some metaphorical beasts from the alchemical menagerie.

> Pale & black with false citrine, imperfect white & red,
> The Peacocks feathers in colour gay, the Rainebowe which shall overgoe,
> The spotted panther, the lyon green, the crowes bil blue as lead,
> These shal apeare before thee perfect white, and manie other moe,
> And after the perfect white, gray, false citrine also,
> And after these, then shall apeare the body red invariable,
> Then hast thou a medicine of the thirde order of his owne kinde
> multiplicable.[44]

33 *eg* Bacon 1597: 13.

34 Norton 1975: line 1534.
35 Cited by Read 1939: 73.

36 Read 1939: 147.
37 Artephius 1624: 216.

38 Hopkins 1967: 92–9. For the possible derivation of this word, *see also* Taylor 1951: 49.

39 'Bloomfield's blossoms' in Ashmole 1652: 322.

40 '*Et rubeum quidem elixir, citrinat in infinitum*' in Geber 1541: 269. The verb *citrino* (to make yellow) seems to date from c1250.
41 Read 1939: 146.
42 Read 1939: 68.

43 *Turba* tr Waite 1896: 88.

44 Ripley 1591: sig. K4.

45 Read 1939: 146.

Basil Valentine compares the stages to birds: the black crow or raven, the white swan, the many colours of the rainbow to the peacock, and the red to the phoenix.[45] The green lion devouring the sun is another colourful alchemical image with a number of possible significances in the alchemical processes (see PLATE VIII).

In later alchemical writings, other colours were said to appear between the simple stages of black, white and red. Thomas Norton said that 'rufe (brownish red) and citryne' came between white and red, and all the colours ever seen appeared at some stage in the process.[46] Some authors said that grey followed black, green followed white, orange preceded red, and many colours in quick succession – the famous stage of 'the peacock's tail' or the rainbow – were said to appear before the white elixir was achieved,[47] 'From White into all Colours withouten faile, / Like to the Rainebow or the Peacock's Tayle', as a poem in Ashmole describes the process[48] (see PLATE IX). Nicholas Flamel listed citrine, green, red, yellow and blue preliminary to the white stage, although he seems to think of the peacock's tail as a blue stage between white and red.[49]

46 Norton 1975: lines 1536, 1547–50.

47 Thomas Charnock; Alphonso, King of Portugal in H P 1652: 6; Bacon 1597: 13.
48 'Bloomfield's blossoms' in Ashmole 1652: 321.

49 Flamel 1624: 108, 121.

These colour stages indicated a succession of processes, on which there was even less agreement than on the colours themselves, as the epigraphs to this chapter suggest. Neither was there any real agreement as to how many there were or how long they took. The numbers suggested were often numerologically significant. Some, like Paracelsus, list seven, the days of the week and of Creation. George Ripley and Daniel Mylius list twelve, the number of the months and Pernetty's Dictionnaire lists twelve stages corresponding to the signs of the Zodiac. Thomas Norton's list of fourteen is unusual.[50] These numbers recur also in the various estimates of time the whole process took: seven days like creation, or, as George Ripley said in one of his works, a year, as the sun needs to go through the whole zodiac.[51] Astrological considerations were often considered important in the alchemical process (see PLATES XII and XIII). Nine months, the period of gestation of the human embryo between its conception and birth, was also mentioned.[52] The alchemist Elias told Helvetius that the whole work was ended in four days, although Helvetius pointed out that various philosophers said it was seven or nine months.[53] At the other extreme George Ripley said that it takes a year only to calcine.[54] The periods of time for the various processes were variously estimated. The number forty was biblically significant and scriptural associations of forty with periods of austerity (the Israelites were in the wilderness forty years, Jesus was tempted in the wilderness for forty days), or for that matter the analogous forty days of Lent, may have suggested it as an appropriate period for the black stage of putrefaction or corruption. Forty days was called 'the philosophical month',[55] and poems in Ashmole's Theatrum chemicum said that the black stage took forty days and to reach the

50 See Read 1939: 137.

51 'Mistery of alchymists' in Ashmole 1652: 388.

52 This was already used by Zosimos, Crosland 1962: 20.

53 Helvetius 1670: 67.

54 Ripley 1591: sig. C3.

55 Dorn 1650: sig. Eee.

PLATE IX (opposite) The peacock's tail from Splendor solis.
[BL, Harley MS 3469, f.28]

PLATE X *(above) The stage of the white elixir, a queen*
*or* Rosa alba *(the white rose).*

[BL, Sloane MS 2560, f.14]

PLATE XI *(opposite) The stage of the red elixir, a king*
*or* Rosa rubea *(the red rose).*

[BL, Sloane MS 2560, f.15]

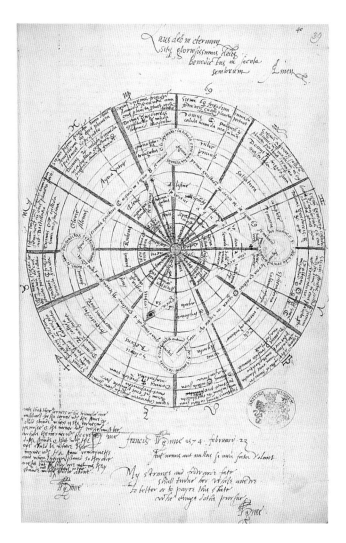

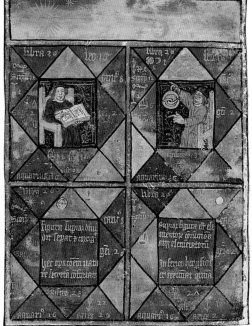

PLATE XII *An astrological-alchemical diagram, made by Francis Thynne, Lancaster Herald (d 1608) and dated 23 February 1574.*

[BL, Additional MS 11,388, f.39]

PLATE XIII *Alchemical horoscopes from the end of Thomas Norton,* Ordinal of alchemy.

[BL, Additional MS 10,302, f.67v]

56 'Bloomfield's
blossoms', in Ashmole
1652: 321.
57 Taylor 1951: 104.

white stage another forty.[56] In Ripley's vision the toad became black and
stood rotting for eighty days and Thomas Norton stayed with his master
forty days learning the art.[57]

There was however some general consensus on the stages and their order,
although various descriptions of subsidiary processes within these large divisions reveal a disagreement between the alchemists that was even more
marked:

(a) breaking down or purification
(b) the preparation or treatment of the resultant material thus purified or
    reduced, which was usually conceived of as separation then joining
    together, alternations between 'body' and 'spirit' or the 'fixed'* and the
    'volatile'*, or numerous repetitions of any or all of these
(c) the production of the white elixir which would transmute metals into
    silver
(d) the production of the red elixir which would transmute metals to gold
(e) augmentation of the potency of the red elixir
(f) projection or transmutation, when the medicine was applied to imperfect
    metals instantly transforming them to gold.

The first stage was signalled by black, and white and red obviously corresponded with the production of those elixirs. There was some agreement that
all processes up to the production of the red elixir should take place in a glass
vessel which would show the colour stages and which should be literally
hermetically sealed and not opened until the red stage was achieved, fixed
and invariable. The matter in the vessel was then put through various pro-

58 'Hunting of the
greene lyon' Ashmole
1652: 285.

cesses signalled by colour changes. Moderate heat, 'an easy fyre',[58] imitating
the temperate and gradual processes of nature, was thought appropriate to
reach the white stage, and a stronger heat, some said double the first heat,
was then applied until the work achieved the unvarying and beautiful red
which signalled success.

The first stage was a preparation of the matter of the Stone. This was
conceived of as either purification or destruction: a washing or a breaking
down of whatever substance had been selected into *prima materia*, the first
matter, which would then subsequently be processed into the Stone. In the
case of purification, waters, salts, acids or sharp liquids (vinegar, urine) were
recommended. The preparation of metals was by processes of purification
and cleansing, removing the earthly superfluities of metals or their 'foul-
ness'. There are various processes to be gone through, eg calcination* and
sublimation*, in these cleansing operations. Mercury, for example, may be
cleansed in a simple process by adding vinegar to it in a glass or stone bowl,
putting it on a mild heat and stirring it with the fingers until it turns bluish
when its colour is a sign of perfect washing, its earthiness having been

59 Geber 1991: 538–9.

washed out with the vinegar.[59] The first stage for Geber is cleansing, either
with the aid of purifying substances such as salt, sal ammoniac*, copperas*
and vinegar which have themselves already been purified by distillation,

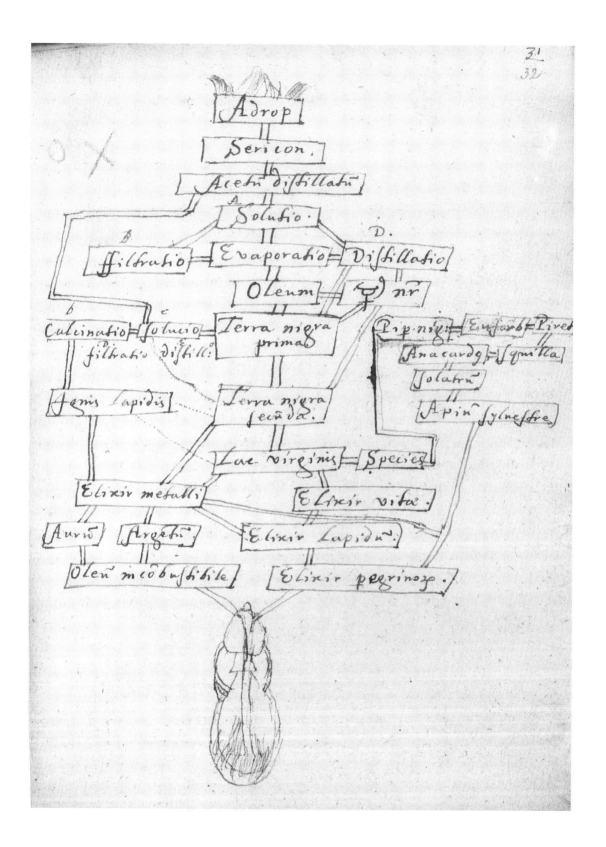

60 Geber, *De
investigatione* in Geber
1928: 7–11.
61 Alphonso King of
Portugal in H P 1652,
cited Read 1939: 137.

calcination and coagulation*, or by fire.[60] In the case of the process of breaking down, the first substance was to be reduced to liquid, 'turned againe into
moistnesse',[61] in accordance with Aristotle's dictum that originally metals
'are in a sense water' (*see above*, p.50). Alternatively the breaking down was
accomplished by heat, thus producing ashes.

The stages between the preparation of the *prima materia* and its transformation into the white elixir were described as many and various, and there
was no real detailed consensus here. All alchemical processes were governed
by the idea of improving or making matter more refined or subtle. Concepts
such as 'exaltation'*, 'elevation'* and 'making noble' appear in the definitions of many processes such as sublimation and distillation in the later
alchemical dictionaries. Even stages such as dissolution and putrefaction*,
which might be thought of as degradations of matter, were seen as temporary
regressions, clearly necessary as the seed must rot and the body die before
new growth and a glorious resurrection. Geber gives a comparatively brief
summation of the work in one chapter: first sublimation and cleansing to
subtilize the raw material of the stone (*ie* mercury) and to make it volatile,
then fixation, and then iterated processes to make the substance in turn

62 Geber 1991: 627–30.

volatile, fixed, soluble, volatile and fixed again.[62] The idea of change is
central to alchemy and one sometimes has the impression that *any* succession
of alternations and changes will do: the hardening of soft bodies or the
softening of hard, fixing the fugitive or making volatile the fixed. In one
passage Geber recommends a series of bewildering alternations between the
'fixed' and the 'volatile': 'by means of sublimination make the fixed stone
volatile, and the volatile fixed, the fixed soluble, and again the soluble
volatile, and then once more the volatile fixed' (*ut iam dudum fixum lapidem
cum modis sublimationis volatilem facias et volatilem fixum et fixum solutum et
solutum iterato volatilem, et iterato volatilem fixum*).[63] Repetition of processes

63 Geber 1991: 629.

results in an increase in the medicine's virtue, as Ben Jonson's alchemist
Subtle knew, 'For look, how oft I iterate the work, / So many times, I add

64 Jonson 1991: II iii
106–7.
65 Bacon, *Opus minus*,
Bacon 1859: 314.
66 Reading *primo in
contritionibus* in
Gratarolus 1561: 81. The
English translation by
Sister Virginia Heines,
Albertus Magnus 1958,
gives 'collecting' as the
first stage, presumably
translating the reading
*primo in contributionibus*
in the Borgnet edition,
1890–9: xxxvii 549.
67 Norton 1975: lxxi.
68 H P 1652: 51.

unto his virtue'.[64] In the thirteenth century Roger Bacon, in a genuine work,
lists pulverisation, solidification, solution, ascension* and distillation
(*depressio*), then a mixing and melting followed by sublimation, attrition,
mortification and distillation. He concludes that anyone knowing how to do
these things would have the perfect medicine which the philosophers call the
elixir.[65] Albertus Magnus gives seven stages: first breaking-down,[66] then
sublimation, fixation, calcination, solution, distillation and coagulation.
Arnold's *Rosarium* lists solution, purification, reduction and fixation,[67] but
the order according to Florianus Raudorff was dissolution, separation, sublimination, fixation or congelation, calcination, ingression.[68] Ripley, in his
'Letter to Edward IV', advises 'First Calcine, and after that Putrefye, / Dys-

*Fig. 29 Diagram from a 16th century MS showing some of the materials and stages (including
solution*, evaporation, distillation and calcination) involved in producing the various elixirs.*
*[BL, Harley MS 2411, f.32]*

69 Ashmole 1652: 115.

70 *primus error in hac arte est festinatio*, Bonus 1546: f.143v.

71 Thomas Charnock' The breviary of naturall philosophy' in Ashmole 1652: 292.

72 *eg* 'Bloomfield's blossoms' in Ashmole 1652: 321.

73 Charnock, 'The breviary of naturall philosophy' in Ashmole 1652: 293–5.
74 *Speculum alchimiae* in Geber 1541: 265,

75 Ripley 1591: sig Gv.

76 Alphonso King of Portugal in H P 1652: 4.
77 John Sawtre in H P 1652: 28.

solve, Dystill, Sublyme, Descende, and Fyxe',[69] but the twelve 'gates' in the *Compound* are calcination, dissolution, separation, conjunction, putrefaction, congelation, cibation*, sublimation, fermentation, exaltation, multiplication, and projection. However, these processes are still roughly grouped according to the general order suggested above, and if there was any agreement in these successions of lengthy and complicated processes it was only that 'in this Art, the chief error is haste'.[70]

In the manufacture of both elixirs, great attention was paid to the fire, which 'if thou knowest not how to governe and keepe, / Thou wert as good go to bed and sleepe',[71] and of which there were various kinds and degrees. In kind there was a major binary division into dry heat, *ie* ordinary fire with several degrees of heat, and moist heat, *ie* heat produced by the water bath (*balneum Mariae*, the bath of Mary, the early alchemist Maria Prophetissa to whom the invention was ascribed), or horse dung, often euphemistically styled *venter equinum* (the horse's stomach). In degree, heat could range, in terms of commonplace alchemical analogies, from the warmth produced by a brooding hen,[72] to summer heat in Egypt, through the degrees of heat of the Sun in the fiery zodiac triplicity of Aries, Leo and Sagittarius. Four degrees of heat – according to some authorities, water, ashes, sand and flame – were likened to the four seasons of the year. Continual and even heat was important – and troublesome and expensive, as Thomas Charnock complains.[73] 'Cook, cook, cook – and don't tire of it', urged Roger Bacon.[74]

Equally important and equally debated was the nature of the vessel(s)* for the work. Alchemists were fond of the axiom that just as the work and its matter were one, so only one vessel was needed, 'One thing, one glasse, one furnace, and no more', as George Ripley declared.[75] After all, to use a popular alchemical analogy, the chick develops inside the one shell. The vessel should be round like the firmament. A glass sphere with a long neck, no thicker than can be grasped with one hand, was advised by Alphonso, King of Portugal.[76] John Sawtre advised 'a Cucurbit* or Gourd with a Limbeck, round above and beneath'.[77] But projection of the elixir on base metal usually took place in a different vessel, the crucible*, in which the imperfect metal to be changed had been made molten.

The perfected Red Elixir was capable of transmuting base metals into gold, but its potency was sometimes then increased in a further stage by multiplication or fermentation (*see above*, p.54, on the Elixir as a ferment). The Elixir was further refined by reiterated sublimations or added to precious metals or mercury, which it leavened like yeast until the whole material was capable of transmutation and was also augmented in its strength. Multiplication meant that the proportion of Stone to base metal in transmutation could be geometrically increased to 1:10, 1:100 or 1:1000, or infinitely. The

*Fig. 30 An alchemical furnace containing a still.*
[BL, Sloane MS 320, f.130v]

Distillation

First ye matter must be dystillid into a lyȝtly spirit, by an vapor & naturall heat, untill ye bodis or matter apere as blacke as pytche, wᵗ is called putrefaction; & yᵉ beware ye burne not ye substance, when he is come & his blackenes & sphere call hym yᵉ toade of ye eorthe or ye dragon's heade—

Alteration or cooperation

After putrefaction, yᵗ is after yᵉ matter is putrified or ye bodis dissolvid, these bodis ar in you clad goth an other bodis by alteration of yᵉ 4 elements, wᵗ is called ye spirituall bodis, drawen out of ye spirituall composition, departid from ye corruptible substance—

Coagulation

Then by his naturall heat & workings he shall alter & change colors & ye forth white, for then he is called vnto Luna, but over ye first white apere, many other colors shall show openlye, ye wᵗ lat passe, but above all monitions take good hede of ye fyer, yᵗ he be no greater ne no hyer then yᵗ ye mayst suffer thi hande betwen yᵉ fyer & ye vessell as it were ye hotest dayes ye somer—

When ye matter is attayned to perfect white then be ye most dilligent that ye fyer not increasinge hygh, but by degrees, nor yet decreasinge, by ye wᵗ meanes he shall not show his whitenes & will show hym self yellow wᵗ color is imperfect, but sordely after he hath showed hym self yellow, he will attayned vnto perfect redness, then is ꝰ turned into ☉, and hath ye power, to turne matter vnto his owne kynde, for then he is come vnto his owne composition & is permanent & hath power to congeall mercurie into his owne kynde as is sayd before &c &c

¶ Sublyme is yᵗ is purgid or puryfyed wᵗ salt or vinegar or distilled from his saltish dregs & feces

¶ Crude is yᵗ wᵗ is rawe & quick comynge wᵗout any thinge mynglyd ꝑto, or distilled from feces

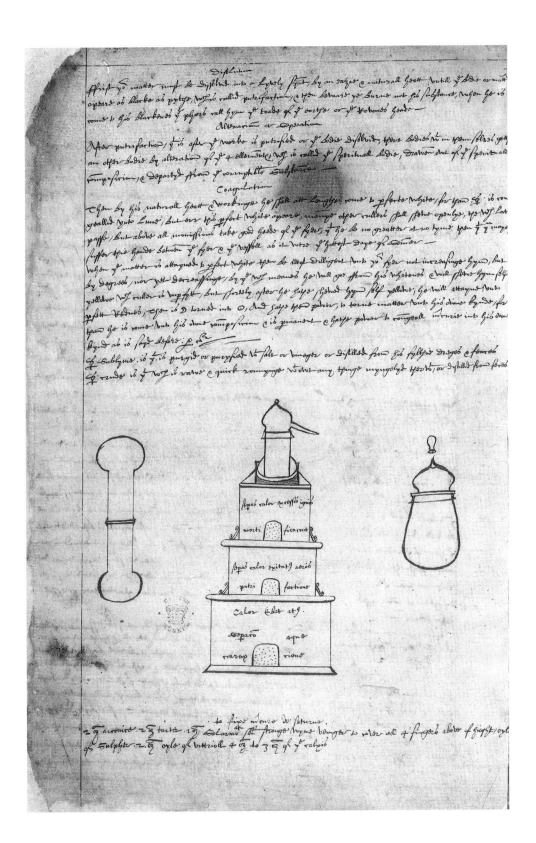

Sepã color a crefto ignio

morti ficaciõ

Sepã color excitã aerio

putri factiõe

Calor est at 9.

separo    aqu̇o

racuỹ    rious

to fixe mercur̃ de Saturno.

2 ℥ arcenic̃ 2 ℥ tarte 1 ℥ Calcino &c strong wyne beinge to colo̅ all 4 fingers above ye hiȝht, oȝl ℥ Sulphur 2 ℥ oyle of vitriall 4 ℥ to 3 ℥ of ye calcyn̄

78 Helvetius 1667: 41.

79 Norton 1975: lines
1083–4.
80 *Rosarium* quoted in H
P 1652: sig. A4.
81 Arnold of Villanova
in *Flos florum* and Geber,
according to *Aureus
tractatus* in *Musaeum
Hermeticum* 1678: 8–9;
Ripley, according to H P
1652: sig A4.
82 Taylor 1951: 44–5.

83 Bacon 1591: 5.
84 Norton 1975: line
1057.
85 The Arabic alchemist
Ibn Umail also rejected
eggs, hair, dung, wine,
blood, bile and sperm,
Crosland 1962: 12.
86 In H P 1652: 17–18; cf
'The Argument of
Morien and Merlin',
Taylor 1948: lines 43–50.
87 Ashmole 1652: 259.

88 Bacon 1597:6.

89 Bacon, *Speculum
alchimiae* in Geber 1541:
260.

90 *Turba* tr Waite 1896:
28, 54.

91 Bacon in Geber 1541:
265. In the *Ordinal*
Norton attributes this
dictum, '*ignis et azogo* [ie
*azoth*] *tibi sufficiunt*' to
Hermes, Norton 1975:
line 2634. It is also to be
found in the treatise by
Morienus.

92 Geber, *De
investigatione perfectionis*
in Geber 1545: 2–3.

93 Thorndike 1923–58:
iii 58.

94 Pereira 1989: 39.

final operation was projection when the Stone was added to molten metal, usually mercury, and instantaneously changed it to gold; in the incident Helvetius reports, accompanied by a certain amount of noise.[78]

But what ought to be the substance(s) selected to be first worked on? 'For many auctours write of that dowte (puzzle), / But none of them shewith it clere owte'.[79] Ought the alchemical process to start on one substance or a combination? Just as the vessel ought to be one,[80] so many treatises repeat the axiom that the matter of the work too is one thing.[81] If this was so, what was that one thing? Although some earlier alchemists, like Geber, seem to entertain the idea that animal or vegetable substances might yield up the Stone, and the early Greek texts solemnly record at least two recipes for the distillation of an egg,[82] later alchemists strenuously reject any first material that is not mineral. Bacon rejects, in passing, blood, hair, urine, excrement and eggs,[83] and similar lists, 'heere, in eggis, in merdis, & uryne',[84] seem to be conventional catalogues of absurd raw materials in later writers.[85] Another much repeated alchemical axiom was that like produced like. The elder-tree does not produce pears, thorns pomegranates, or thistles figs says *The book of John Sawtre*,[86] and *The worke of John Dastin* is not alone in pointing out that man engenders man and beast beast.[87] So some authorities suggested gold itself, as the purest metal, might be thought to be nearest in nature to the Elixir which would eventually transmute all metals into gold. Others pointed out that even if gold were the most perfect metal, that perfection in itself was not sufficient to help imperfect metals to perfection.[88] Alternatively gold was thought to contain the first principles of mercury and sulphur in the purest forms. Bacon argues that nothing other than these two are able to bring them to perfection or transmute them, and hence mercury and sulphur are 'the matter of our stone'.[89] Others thought mercury, as the 'mother' of all metals ought to be the starting point. The suggestion at various points in the *Turba philosophorum*, which perhaps preserves traces of older ideas, of copper and lead as metals to work on, is untypical.[90] The general tendency of thought in Geber is that the 'medicines' of metals ought to be elicited from mercury: 'Fire and azoth* (mercury) are enough for you' declared Bacon,[91] in a much-quoted maxim. So, not only is mercury one of the raw materials of all metals, it is also the raw material of the agent which will eventually help less perfect metals on their journey to being gold, the most perfect combination of mercury and sulphur.

Alternatively, the elixir itself, like metals, is prepared from nothing other than mercury and sulphur,[92] or, in a further theoretical refinement, mercury was thought to contain within itself an internal sulphur. This stress on the greater importance of mercury, and the idea that gold could be made from mercury alone, seems to have prevailed in the fourteenth and fifteenth centuries, and is found in Arnald of Villanova (*see* Chapter 2, p.38).[93] Arnald is supposed to have claimed that 'I would transmute (*tingerem*) the sea, if it were mercury'.[94] In any case the task of breaking down the chosen substance was to produce 'our mercury' for *nostrum argentum vivum non est argentum vivum vulgi* ('our mercury is not the mercury of the common people'), as the alchemists never seemed to tire of saying. It was also called the 'philosophers' mercury', or as Ripley put it 'But not the common called quicksilver by name'.[95] Alternatively the intention of the initial dissolution into prime matter was to produce 'our mercury' and 'our sulphur', Aristotle's first principles of metals. A black colour, and sometimes a foul and stinking smell, indicated that the material had been successfully broken down and the long and complicated and repetitive journey to the achievement of the Stone could continue on its way to 'perfect ruby'.

95 Ripley 1591: sig. B4.

*Fig. 31 A male and female alchemist enjoin silence at the end of the (almost wordless) book the* Mutus liber. *J J Manget,* Bibliotheca chemica curiosa *(2 vols Cologne 1702).*
[BL, 44.i.11, 12, i, plate 14]

# CHAPTER 4

# THE LANGUAGES OF ALCHEMY

When the sages said in this Art that [the Stone's] nature is worthless and it is sold for little, they caused common people to err. For they said that its nature is more precious than all other natures, yet with this statement they deceived many people and yet spoke the truth.

*Turba philosophorum* in *Auriferae artis*

Now to unriddle this mystery and to propose truthes in ciphers, though they are obscure, yet by them you may learne, and shall finde they are no vaine things; and if thou commest to understand this great Mystery, have it not in thy ordinary conversation, but leave it in the same cipher ....

*Treatise of Alphonso king of Portugal*, tr.H P

Their chiefest study was to wrap up their Secrets in Fables, and spin out their Fancies in Vailes and shadowes, whose Radii seem to extend every way, yet so, that they all meete in a Common Center, and point onely at One thing.

Ashmole, *Theatrum chemicum Britannicum*

But all I say is false, therefore I say nothing true ... but when I say 'true', understand 'false'.

[pseudo-] Bacon, *Sanioris medicinae*

Thou hast done nothing but pile up ambiguous words. Return, therefore, to the subject.

Response of the 'Crowd of Philosophers' to Bocascus, *Turba philosophorum*, tr. Waite

From its beginnings alchemy was partly concerned with material practices which aimed at producing change in substances, especially minerals. Alchemists also concerned themselves with theory and speculation, often in figurative language. Roger Bacon (for once, the real one) wrote of two sorts of alchemy: *alkimia operativa* which teaches the making of the noble metals, and another alchemy, a speculative art.[1] For this reason, as in the case of music up to the Renaissance, one species of alchemical treatise was divided into theory (*theorica*) and practice (*practica*, that is, practical instructions, or collections of recipes); examples of the latter are the *Practica* of Rasis, Michael Scot's *Alchimia*, Albert's *Alkimia minor* and John of Rupescissa's *Liber lucis*.[2] Some treatises contain an internal division into *theorica* and *practica*, for example Arnald's *Rosarium*, Lull's *Testament* and the alchemical

1 Bacon 1859: i 39–40.

2 *See* Halleux 1979: 80.

poem 'Bloomfield's blossoms' in Ashmole's *Theatrum*. One recent writer on

3 Halleux 1979: 73.

alchemy has divided its writings into receipts, theoretical and practical treatises, *summae*, allegories, and exegesis.[3] An added complication is that it is not always clear whether the allegories occupying some or all of some alchemical treatises are figurative expressions concealing practical processes from the vulgar, and revealing them through a veil to the initiate, or whether the medium is the message and the allegory is meant to reveal some other meaning. One of the things that sharply divides alchemy from chemistry is that from the earliest times the instructions for practical craft operations and chemical processes went hand in hand with figurative expression and elaborate metaphorical language. Writers on alchemy used language in ways that were not exclusively, and perhaps not even primarily, confined to expressing the production of change in metals. And although early definitions of alchemy concentrate on the making of noble metals (for example those of Suidas or Albert Magnus), alchemy has always contained what Halleux calls

4 Halleux 1979: 47–9.

'motifs idéologiques' and from its beginnings is thus constituted by 'un ensemble de pratiques et de spéculations'.[4] If one factor common to alchemy and chemistry is technique, then perhaps the use of language is one of the things that marks their difference.

For all these reasons the discourses of alchemy are actually an obstacle to those wishing to extract chemical procedures from alchemical writings or to trace genuine chemical reactions in their descriptions. As Jung pointed out,

> from the point of view of our modern knowledge of chemistry it [alchemy] tells us little or nothing, and if we turn to the texts with their hundred and one procedures and recipes left behind by the Middle Ages and Antiquity, we shall find relatively few among them with any recognizable meaning for the

5 Jung, *Psychology and alchemy* cited in Debus, 'Significance' 1965: 43.

> chemist.[5]

In the light of these uses of language, the debate about which is more important in alchemy – the chemical process in the laboratory or any esoteric, psychological or religious significance – may be seen as fruitless. F. Sherwood Taylor's beautifully balanced comment on alchemical language, 'the

5 Taylor 1951: 160.

expression of the perfecting of matter in terms of human experience',[6] discloses discourses where the material and metaphorical worlds had not yet parted company, and in which both a metal and a human being had body,

7 *See* Chapter 3, p.51.

soul and spirit.[7] The alchemists themselves were aware of the infinite number of discourses, metaphors and analogies that alchemy could appropriate. As Petrus Bonus says, the Stone may be compared, by analogy, with

8 Petrus Bonus 1546: f.52.

all things in the world: creation, animals, vegetables, conception and death.[8]

It may prove useful to think of alchemy's languages in four ways: its characteristic use of language and the 'rhetoric' of alchemy; its narratives; other discourses which (to use alchemical metaphors) it 'amalgamated' or perhaps 'fermented', and its recurrent images and metaphors.

Alchemy was from its origins a secret art. Even the earliest Greek texts contain synonyms, symbols and codes, such as Zosimos's formula of the crab.

*Fig. 32 Alchemical symbols for substances, apparatus and processes from a 17th century collection of alchemical tracts in Italian.*

[BL, Additional MS 10,766, f.9]

*Fig. 33 (below, left) Alchemical symbols.*

[BL, Sloane MS 3772, f.44v]

*Fig. 34 (below, right) Alchemical symbols. Johannes Conrad Barchusen,* Elementa chemiae *(Leyden 1718).*

[BL, 1034.h.10, sig. Yyy3]

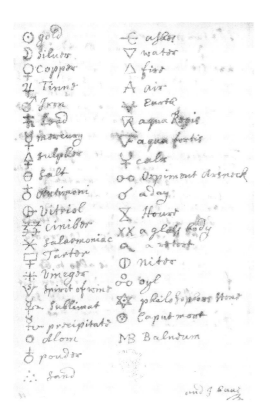

### Signorum apud Chemicos usitatorum explicatio.

| | | | |
|---|---|---|---|
| + | Acetum | ♃ { | Jupiter |
| ※ | Acetum destillatum | | Stannum |
| △ | Aër | ♎ | Libra |
| O | Alumen | MB | Mariæ Balneum |
| aaa | Amalgama | ⊠ | Mensis |
| aa | ana. i. e. recensitorum pars æqualis | ☿ { | Mercurius |
| ♁ | Antimonium | | Hydrargyrum |
| ∴ | Arena | | Argentum vivum |
| ☾ { | Argentum | ⊕ | Nitrum |
| | Luna | ♂ | Nox |
| ▽ | Aqua | ♄ { | Plumbum |
| ▽F | Aqua fortis | | Saturnus |
| ▽R | Aqua Regia | ♂♂ | Oleum |
| ☉ { | Aurum | ⇌ | Præcipitare |
| | Sol | ℞ | Recipe |
| ⊶ | Auripigmentum | ↶ | Retorta |
| ⊶ | Arsenicum | ⊖ | Sal |
| Ψ | Calx viva | ⊖∧ | Sal alkali fixum |
| ♋ | Cancer | ⊖∨ | Sal alkali volatile |
| ☉ | Caput mortuum | Ə | Scrupulus |
| ♋♋ | Cinnabaris | Ɔ | Spiritus |
| -E | Cineres clavellati | ⩘ | Spiritus vini |
| C.C. | Cornu Cervi | S.S.S. | Stratum super stratum |
| ♀ { | Cuprum | ⌫ | Sublimare |
| | Æs | ♠ | Sulphur |
| | Venus | ⊓ | Tartarus |
| ✠ { | Crucibulum | Tᴿ | Tinctura |
| | Tigillum | ▽ | Terra |
| ♌ | Destillare | VB | Vaporis Balneum |
| ♂ | Dies | ⊕ { | Viride æris |
| 3 | Drachma | | Ærugo |
| ♂ { | Ferrum | ⊕ | Vitriolum |
| | Chalybs | ⨯⨯ { | Vitrum |
| | Mars | | Alembicus |
| 8 | Hora | ℥ | Uncia |
| △ | Ignis | ⊡ | Urina |

9 Norton 1975: line 54.

Alchemical codes were not only manifested in ciphers and symbols for processes and substances, but in the very way the alchemists wrote. Obscurity of expression was often intentional, for the secrets of God were being touched on, and direct revelation was sin. The science was sacred and secret, 'the subtle science of holi Alchymye' as Norton calls it,[9] and the art was not for the common people.

There is a strong tradition in western thought that important truths are most properly expressed in a veiled, obscure or difficult way. This, said some, is why Christ spoke in parables. Alchemical adapts too formulated their sayings in parables (*locuti sunt de eis per similitudinem*),[10] the philosophers in past times spoke 'as in a riddle, or with a cloudy voice',[11] and their 'noble practice doth hem [*ie* alchemists] teach / To vaile their secrets with mistie speach'.[12] Alchemists were aware of the cryptic quality of earlier authorities who wrote before them, and often comment on it. Many promise, therefore, to write clearly: hardly any do. Albert the Great undertakes, encouragingly, at the beginning of his *Libellus de alchima* to write for his friends in a way clear and free from error, but the same sentence goes on, 'in such a way that seeing, they will not see, and hearing, will not understand'.[13] Petrus Bonus, the author of the treatise *Pretiosa margarita novella*, writes clearly, or so his editor Janus Lacinius claims, and is unlike those who bewilder the enquirer, and whose books of alchemy are full of obscurity and poetical fables.[14] Indeed Lacinius fears that the *Pretiosa margarita* may be *too* clear. Of course, he need not have worried.

10 'Book of Morienus' ed Stavenhagen 1974: 12.
11 Bacon, *Speculum alchimiae* in Geber 1541: 257.
12 'Hunting of the greene lyon' in Ashmole 1652: 278.

13 Albertus Magnus in Gratarolus 1561: 79. The text deliberately echoes the words of Christ on the obscurity of parables, Luke 8: 10.

14 Petrus Bonus 1546: sig. *4 and f. 6.

One way in which alchemy was encoded in language was in the use of riddling expressions, such as when Basil Valentine tells us that the Stone is derived from two things and one thing, in which is concealed the third thing.[15] It also uses enigma and paradox, figures of *aequivocationis, allegoriae et metaphorae* as Petrus Bonus puts it, admitting that if you stripped the figures of speech from treatises the remainder '*in octo vel duodecim lineis scribere . . . possent*' ('could be written down in some eight or twelve lines'),[16] and thus voicing one of the well-worn paradoxes of alchemy, that in essence the theory, practice and accomplishment of the art of alchemy were brief.

15 Coudert 1980: 63.

16 Petrus Bonus 1546: f.48v.

The riddling and oracular style, and also brevity, characterise the maxims of the 'Emerald Table' of Hermes Trismegistus,[17] which may be one of the oldest Arabo-Latin texts[18] and was perhaps translated into Latin some time around 1200.[19] It was revered and quoted by later alchemists, and was said to have been found in Hermes' hands in his tomb, or discovered by Sara the wife of Abraham, or by Alexander the Great.[20] It is a series of gnomic utterances which were much quoted and commented on, notably by Ortulanus, whose commentary, often found in manuscripts or printed books after the

17 On other treatises ascribed to Hermes in the middle ages *see* Thorndike 1923–58: ii 214–28.
18 Halleux 1979: 83.
19 Taylor 1951: 90.
20 *See* Holmyard 1957: 95–8; *Turba* ed Ruska 1931.

*Fig. 35 Hermes Trismegistus points to the sun and moon, the subjects of the fourth dictum from the 'Emerald Table', which is here varied in the motto. Michael Maier,* Symbola aureae mensae *(Frankfurt 1617).*
[BL, 90.i.25, p. 5]

# I HERMETIS ÆGY-
## PTIORVM REGIS ET AN-
### TESIGNANI SYMBOLVM.

*SOL EST EIVS CONIVGII PATER ET*
*alba Luna Mater, tertius succedit, vt*
*gubernator, Ignis.*

Rimarium apud Auream Menſam locum
HERMETI ÆGYPTIO, tanquam proregi
& Vicario ſuo Regia virgo CHEMIA depu-
tauit & attribuit, vt iam antè commemora-
uimus,

A 3

Table, makes its utterances more rather than less obscure. Its first four maxims are as follows:

> True it is, without falsehood, certain and most true.
> That which is above is like to that which is below, and that which is below is like to that which is above, to accomplish the miracles of one thing.
> And as all things were by the contemplation of one, so all things arose from this one thing by a single act of adaptation.
> The father thereof is the Sun, the Mother the moon . . .[21]

21 Holmyard 1957: 95, citing the tr by R Steele and D W Singer.

Alchemical discourse is particularly fond of paradox. Zosimos was already using paradox to describe the agent of transmutation ('a stone but not a stone, a stone unknown and known to all', *see above* Chapter 1, p.21), in motifs which were repeatedly endlessly in later alchemical literature. In part this was an extension of the idea of a secret language in which the adepts' truth was really the opposite of the ordinary sense of the words. So alchemy insists that 'our' water, sulphur or lead, or the mercury or vinegar of the philosophers are quite different from the substances usually signified by those names. The prefix *noster* [our] before a noun or the suffix *philosophorum* [of the philosophers] after it usually signal a paradox in alchemical discourse. Our stone was not a stone, our water was a dry water, and 'the lead of the philosophers' was gold. In a starkly paradoxical entry for mercury in Martin Rulandus' alchemical dictionary, we find one of the two principles of metals signified by the other: '*mercurius, id est sulphur*'.[22]

22 Rulandus 1612: 331.

Paradox is used in many discourses to express transcendent value. In religious language, the despised and rejected is *therefore* precious. Medieval mystics said that the most appropriate way of thinking about divine things was in the most dissimilar terms we can imagine, thus we may clearly recognise the impossibility of attempting to represent the divine accurately. Thomas Aquinas, commenting on one of the Epistles said that 'vile things' (*corpora vilia*) are particularly apt as representations of the Deity.[23] In Shakespeare's *King Lear* the King of France uses paradox rightly to assay the unique worth of Cordelia,

23 Aquinas 1966: 161–2.

> Fairest Cordelia, that art most rich, being poor;
> Most choice, forsaken; and most lov'd despised!
> Thee and thy virtues here I seize upon;
> Be it lawful I take up what's cast away.

The unique worth of the Stone, conceived of by alchemists as the most precious of things, particularly attracted paradox, and it was consequently also described as mean, unnoticed and most ordinary, 'noble and worthless, valuable and of small account',[24] or even as the vilest of things, found in refuse or on the dunghill. The treatise *Gloria mundi* describes the stone in this same way:

24 *Tractatus aureus* in *Musaeum Hermeticum* 1678: 10.

> [The Stone] is found in the country, in the village, in the town, in all things created by God; yet it is despised by all. Rich and poor handle it every day. It is cast into the street by servant maids. Children play with it. Yet no one prizes it, though, next to the human soul, it is the most beautiful and precious thing

25 *Gloria mundi* in *Musaeum Hermeticum* tr Waite 1893: i 180.

26 'scias quod radix eius sit una, et rcs una atque una substancia' and 'azoc et ignis in hac compositione tibi sufficient', Stavenhagen 1974: 12, 32. 'Bloomfield's blossoms' too says the Stone is made from one substance, in one vessel and in one operation, Ashmole 1652: 319.
27 *Turba* tr Waite 1896: 57.
28 Ripley 1591: sig E4v.

29 Fragment, Ashmole 1652: 436.
30 John Dastin cited in Holmyard 1967: 147.
31 Stavenhagen 1974: 34.
32 Commentary of Hortulanus in Geber 1541: 368.

33 Ashmole 1652: 407, 409.

34 Petrus Bonus 1546: f.115V.

35 *Turba* tr Waite 1896: 31.

36 Crosland 1962: 66.

37 H P 1652: 1.

38 Helvetius 1670: 45–6, 54.
39 Flamel 1624: 23.

upon earth, and has power to pull down kings and princes. Nevertheless, it is esteemed the vilest and meanest of earthly things. It is cast away and rejected by all.[25]

Alchemists persisted with the claim, whether with conviction or as a concealing rhetorical ploy is difficult to tell, that the manufacture of the Stone was simple and that the operation has one root, one matter and one substance, and that mercury and fire are all that are needed.[26] Consequently both paradox, in the particular sense of expressing thc complex as simple, and the assertion of the simple unity of alchemy, meant that the alchemists sometimes use deliberately homely language and comparisons. So the making of the Stone, or at least some of its stages, is like 'the work of women and the play of children' as the alchemists are fond of asserting. 'Socrates' in the *Turba philosophorum* is one of the earliest to voice this idea, in his assertion of the simplicity of the Work after the white stage.[27]

Ripley anticipates the white stage by saying that when the children's shirts are filled with piss the woman will wash them,[28] or 'Let the old man drinke wine till he pisse', as a fragment of an alchemical poem in Ashmole advises.[29] Similarly the process could be compared to homely procedures: yeast fermenting, the making of cheese or bread.[30] The fermentation of gold is like that of bread,[31] for leaven nourishes and ferments a great quantity of dough, converting it into its own substance.[32] Grind down the first matter to powder like a miller, advises an anonymous poem in Ashmole's *Theatrum*, which demands for a later alchemical process that the alchemist learn the baker's trade and 'how he Leavens Bread by Fermentacion'.[33] The second part of the Work requires the right moment, just as when you are baking bread or sweetmeats [*ut panis et confectiones de melle et de zuccaro*][34] and Haly compares the preparation to that of soap. Mix, cook and simmer advises Arisleus in the *Turba*.[35] Some homely terms, such as 'washing' and 'roasting' are still used by twentieth-century chemists.[36]

Narratives in alchemical treatises are vivid, surreal and dream-like, and tend generically to romance. Some are literally dream-like as they are in the form of dream-visions, such as Ripley's allegorical vision of the toad in his *Compound*, and 'Bloomfield's blossoms' and the dream-vision of John Dastin, both in Ashmole's *Theatrum*. Alchemical works display recurrent narrative motifs, such as learning the art from an adept, often a learned and exotic stranger: Alphonso, King of Portugal sent for an adept to Egypt,[37] Elias the artist who visited Helvetius was about 44, mysterious, of middling height and pockmarked, and had himself learned the secret of transmutation from a friend.[38] Nicholas Flamel had to have the aid of the Spanish Jew, Master Canches, to interpret the book of Abraham the Jew,[39] and many English alchemists tell tales of instruction by adepts.

Other alchemical narratives are violent and disturbing and recount conflict, warfare, murder, sex, and violence. Torture is already a motif in the visions of Zosimos, with their accounts of mutilation, boiling and dismemberment, which attracted the attention of Jung. The advice of the *Turba* too

EMBLEMA III. *De ſecretis Naturæ.*

Vade ad mulierem lavantem pannos, tu fac ſimiliter.

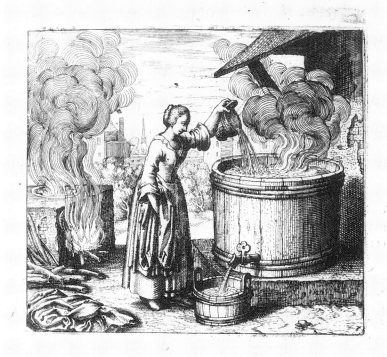

EPIGRAMMA III.

*Abdita quiſquis amas ſcrutari dogmata, ne ſis*
*Deſes, in exemplum, quod juvet, omne trahas:*
*Anné vides, mulier maculis abſtergere pannos*
*Ut ſoleat calidis, quas ſuperaddit, aquis?*
*Hanc imitare, tuâ nec ſic fruſtraberis arte,*
*Námque nigri fæcem corporis unda lavat.*

C 3 S1

*Fig. 36 'Go to the woman washing clothes and do likewise'. Michael Maier,* Atalanta fugiens *(Oppenheim 1617).*
*[BL, 90.i.19, Emblem III, p. 21]*

*Fig. 37 (opposite) The riddle of Oedipus. Michael Maier,* Atalanta fugiens *(Oppenheim 1617).*
*[BL, 90.i.19, Emblem XXXIX, p. 165]*

# Oedypus Sphynge superata & trucidato Lajo patre matrem ducit in uxorem.

# EPIGRAMMA XXXIX.

Sphyngem ænigmatico Thebis sermone timendam
    Oedypus ad propriam torserat arte necem:
Quæsitum est, cui manè pedes sint bis duo, luce
    Sed mediâ bini, tres, ubi vesper adest.
Victor abhinc Lajum nolentem cedere cædit,
    Ducit & uxorem quæ sibi mater erat.    X 3    BA:

40 'corpora diruite &
cruciate, donec
alterentur', Turba in
Auriferae artis 1572: 126.
41 See Duncan 1942: 631.

is to break up bodies and torture them until they are altered,[40] and Mercury complains of torture in Ben Jonson's alchemical masque *Mercury vindicated from the alchemists at court* (1615).[41]

Parricide and incest are often motifs. The myths of classical antiquity are drawn on (*see below*, pp.74–8), such as Saturn's castration of his father or Jupiter's deposition, in turn, of his father Saturn,[42] or the story of Oedipus, which in the twentieth century has preoccupied Freud in psychology and Levi-Strauss in anthropology. New stories are narrated, such as that of parricide and resurrection in the *Pretiosa margarita novella*, in which a king refuses a share of his power to his son, is stabbed, buried, and rots, but his bones 'thicken' and he eventually rises from his tomb.

42 See the illustration of
the castration of Uranus
from the 15th century
Bibliotheca Apostolica
Vaticana, Cod. Pal. lat.
1066 f.226 reproduced in
de Rola 1973.

43 Crosland 1962: 7.

Consequently, one of the discourses appropriated by alchemy was that of the mythology of classical antiquity, and it was particularly after the fifteenth century that writers combined alchemy and classical mythology.[43] Perhaps the absurdity of literal interpretation made allegorical interpretation more plausible. Narratives from classical antiquity were regularly appropriated and interpreted as alchemical allegories, especially (and for obvious

*Typicarum imaginum expositio .*

TRIA in opere seruanda sunt, primo materiá præparâ, secundo opus continuâ, ne discontinuatione dissipetur, tertio sis patiens intima naturæ passim uestigia seruans.

PRAEPARA primo aquam uitæ summæ purificatam, & eâ seruâ. Non tamen credas, ut liquor iste, quo cuncta madent, sit Bacchi candens ac limpidus humor. Nam te dum uarijs immensa per auia rebus, detines intentum, felices præteris undas.

PALATIVM ingredieris in quo quindecim sunt mansiones ubi Rex diademate coronatus in excelsa sede sceptrum totius orbis in manu tenens erit: coram cuius maiestate filius cū quinq; famulis uarijs indutis uestibus, flexis genibus regé deprecantur ut tam filio quàm seruis regnum impertiri dignaretur, quorum precibus nil Rex ipse respondit .

COLLIGIT in tertio loco filius sua ueste patris sanguinem, quod est secundum opus & in Methodo iam declaratum .

At filius

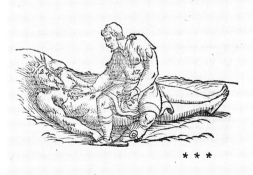

* * *

THE LANGUAGES OF ALCHEMY

reasons) those of the achievement of difficult quests, again suggesting alchemy's affinity with romance narrative. The alchemical myth *par excellence* often referred to in alchemical treatises was of course the story of Jason's achievement of the Golden Fleece, which gave its name to an alchemical treatise the *Aureum vellus* or *Le toison d'or*. The same tenth-century Greek lexicon which gives an early gloss of *chemeia* (*see* p.19) already euhemeristically interpreted (as did Jonson's Sir Epicure Mammon in *The alchemist*[44]) the Fleece as an alchemical treatise written on sheep-skin which gave instructions for gold-making;[45] the seventh-century writer John of Antioch had also made a connection between this myth and alchemy.[46] A desire to interpret myths instructively opened them to allegorical exegesis, as it did to

44 Jonson 1991: II i 89–91.

45 Suidas 1928–38: ii 24.

46 Crosland 1962: 8. *See* also Sandys 1970: 335 and Ashmole 1652: sig. B3.

*Fig. 38 (opposite and below) The old king enthroned and then murdered by his son who collects his blood. He rises from his tomb and shows his power by giving golden crowns to his sons and making them kings in their turn. Petrus Bonus,* Pretiosa margarita novella *(Venice 1546)*
*[BL, G.2314, sigs **8v–*** and sigs ***4-4v]*

ET *ſic alternatim mittuntur Angeli,qui primam, ſecundam,tertiam & quartá partem oſſium proÿciunt, ut ſcilicet albeſcat, ſit lucida atque firmetur . Quinto & ſexto firmata mutetur in citrinum . Et ſic cum ſeptima, octaua & nona parte : oſſium terra efficitur uti ſanguis atque rubinus .*

TVNC *Rex ſurgens,de ſepulcro Dei gratia plenus,factus eſt totus ſpiritus totusq; cœlicus cum poteſtate magna, potens facere Reges omnes ſuos famulos .*

POSTREMO *potentiam ſuam ſuper filium: & ſeruos demonſtrat,eis coronas aureas ſingulas ſingulis imponendo, ut ſint & ipſi Reges gratia ſui, cui dominus dedit poteſtatem magnam atque maieſtatem .*

*Impuris nemo manibus fraudator , auarus , Sacrilegus' ue aliquis pergraue tangat opus . Huc probus , huc ſapiens animo ſe conferat , & qui Cum rerum cauſis dogmata noſſe queat.*

*ATALANTA*
*FVGIENS,*
*hoc est,*

# EMBLEMATA
## NOVA
## DE SECRETIS NATURÆ
### CHYMICA,

Accommodata partim oculis & intellectui, figuris
cupro incisis, adjectisque sententiis, Epigram-
matis & notis, partim auribus & recreationi
animi plus minus 50 Fugis Musicalibus trium
Vocum, quarum duæ ad unam simplicem melo-
diam distichis canendis peraptam, correspon-
deant, non absq; singulari jucunditate videnda,
legenda, meditanda, intelligenda, dijudicanda,
canenda & audienda:

*Authore*

MICHAELE MAJERO Imperial. Con-
sistorii Comite, Med. D. Eq. ex. &c.

*OPPENHEIMII*
Ex typographia HIERONYMI GALLERI,
*Sumptibus* JOH. THEODORI de BRY,

M DC XVII.

readings which extracted significance in natural philosophy, moral philosophy or theology. Other classical myths involving gold offered themselves as candidates for alchemical allegorization: Hercules and the golden apples of the Hesperides, the Ovidian story (*Metamorphoses* X 560–680) of the race between Atalanta and Hippomenes who won both the race and Atalanta by distracting her with golden apples. This story inspired the extraordinary collection of alchemical emblems and musical fugues in Michael Maier's *Atalanta fugiens*, whose engraved title-page illustrates this story and also Hercules and the apples of the Hesperides.

*Fig. 39 (opposite) Alchemical myths. In the left and top margins Hercules accomplishes one of his labours by obtaining the golden apples of the Hesperides despite three guardian nymphs and a dragon. In the right and bottom margins Hippomenes wins the race against Atalanta by distracting her with golden balls thrown in her path. Michael Maier,* Atalanta fugiens *(Oppenheim 1617).*
[BL, 90.i.19, title page]

*Fig. 40 The death of Adonis. Michael Maier,* Atalanta fugiens *(Oppenheim 1617).*
[BL, 90.i.19, Emblem XLI, p. 173]

Other classical myths were interpreted alchemically, especially the tales of transmutation in Ovid's *Metamorphoses*, with its 'dark Philosophie of turned shapes' as Arthur Golding's translation of 1567 called it. Helvetius recalls Ovid generally when he transmuted lead to gold and he has an extended Ovidian mythological rhapsody, including Aeneas, Diana's fountain, the blood of Pyramus and Thisbe, Adonis, and the apotheoses of Romulus, Caesar and Hercules.[47] More generally these myths included the labours of Hercules and Theseus and the Minotaur. An incident in the latter story also gave its name to an alchemical treatise, *Le filet d'Ariadne pour entrer avec seureté dans le labirinthe de la philosophie hermétique*. Jung later thought of his own alchemical-psychological researches in terms of the Theseus story, and wandering in the labyrinth without Ariadne's thread was used as a warning in an alchemical treatise[48] against taking words in their ordinary significance. Nicholas Flamel and others interpreted the black sail Theseus left on his ship, thus causing his father Aegeon's death, as the first black stage of the alchemical process, *putrefactio*.[49] Other myths more obliquely appropriated by alchemy are Sisyphus (the unending task), Daphne's flight from Apollo (the attempted escape of the volatile principle), Oedipus (the riddles of alchemy), Penelope longing for the return of Ulysses (a dry stage of the work in which the matter is denied humidity) and Hercules' cleansing of the Augean stables (successful achievement of the white stage). Alchemists' enthusiasm for classical myths could lead to inaccurate eclecticism, as when Nicholas Flamel talks of Theseus (rather than Jason) sowing the serpent's teeth.[50]

Alchemical discourse was also suffused with the language of Christianity, its ethics, scriptures, liturgy and doctrines. Images of death and resurrection, which for later alchemists prefigured the dissolution of the prime matter and its reconstitution into the glorious Stone, were central to Christian doctrine and also to the mystery religions, both of which provided cultural contexts for the earliest alchemical texts. The language of death and resurrection is present in the visions of Zosimos, who also mentions Jesus Christ as a saviour,[51] and some of the early Greek alchemical texts display the 'redemption motif'.[52] In the eighth century Stephanos of Alexandria used the transformation of metals as an analogy for the transformation of the soul.[53] Later alchemists too thought of metals being redeemed from their 'sins'.

A religious tone is discernible in many alchemical texts and numerous treatises piously invoke God at their beginnings or give him thanks at their ends. A religious and holy life was often thought a prerequisite for a successful alchemist: the alchemist is a divine man and true priest.[54] A personal revelation and the practice of personal morality were recommended by both religion and alchemy. No one may accomplish the work except through affection, humility and love, for it is the gift of God to his humble servants.[55] The art itself is the 'glorious science of God and doctrine of the saints',[56] the study of this art can proceed only from 'a right Noble and Vertuous disposition, and by a Divine instinct' and Hermes himself came to knowledge by the

47 Helvetius 1670: 21–4.

48 Artephius 1624: 196; cf 'such who wanted *Ariadne's* threed in the Labyrinth of Alchemy', 'Marrow of alchemy', Ferguson 1915: 108.
49 Coudert 1980: 141.

50 Flamel 1624: 89.

51 Jung cited in Norton 1975: lviii.
52 Sheppard 1959.
53 Crosland 1962: 10.

54 Pereira 1989: 36.

55 Stavenhagen 1974: 10.

56 Aquinas 1966: 46.

THE LANGUAGES OF ALCHEMY

57 H P sig. A3v.
Trismosin too thought
alchemy a gift from God,
Read 1939: 87.
58 Stavenhagen 1974: 10.
59 Norton 1975: line 186.
60 'Sir Edward Kelle's
worke' in Ashmole 1652:
325.

61 'Bloomfield's
blossoms' in Ashmole
1652: 307.

62 *Aureus tractatus* in
*Musaeum Hermeticum*
1678: 6.

63 Ripley 1591: Epistle
dedicatory, sigs
A4–A4V.

64 Pereira 1989: 87.

Creator's favour.[57] God prepares one to whom the secret may be handed on.[58]
The secrets of alchemy are never merely to be found out by human labour,
but 'bi teching or revelacion'[59] and the Stone is to be obtained by grace,
rather than reading.[60] Like religion, alchemy depended ultimately on divine
revelation. There is a notion of an alchemical 'election' just as there is a
religious one, especially in Calvinism: 'God maketh it sensible, / To some
Elect, to others he doth it denay',[61] and an alchemical treatise may claim to be
perfcctly lucid to those predestined to understand it ('*dignis & a Deo praedesti-
natis*').[62] The Stone is found by the few that have retired from society
in contempt of the world.[63] There are many injunctions to live temperately
(perhaps in imitation of the moderate heat that produces the Stone), and
cleanly (perhaps in imitation of the first alchemical stage of purification). The
incipit of a Lullian work on alchemy declares that a man who 'knows' a
woman actually or in a dream cannot make the Stone.[64] Patience is certainly
necessary.

65 Taylor 1948: lineᶜ
20–21.

66 *Musaeum Hermeticum*
tr Waite 1893: i 57.

67 Aquinas 1966: 132ff.

68 *Musaeum Hermeticum*
1678: 53–72.

Scriptural texts and narratives were appropriated and interpreted
alchemically, as were classical myths. Scripture can give information useful
to the alchemist.[65] One writer found that his eyes were suddenly opened
about stories in the Old Testament, such as the harvest Rachel gave to Leah
and the Golden Calf, as the disciples' were on the road to Emmaus.[66] *Aurora
consurgens*, attributed to Aquinas, has an alchemical interpretation of the
Song of Songs, which it draws on particularly at its end,[67] and the treatise
*Aureum seculum redivivum*[68] is really an extended alchemical fantasia on this
much-interpreted biblical book, reading alchemically figures usually given a
theological interpretation (for example, the beloved as the Virgin Mary or the
Church, the lover as Christ); the cry of the beloved '*nigra sum sed formosa*' (I
am black but comely) is taken as referring to the black stage of the alchemical

69 *Musaeum Hermeticum*
1678: 58.

70 *Musaeum Hermeticum*
1678: 63.
71 Ashmole 1652: 351.

work.[69] '*Aureum seculum redivivum*' even paraphrases the words of Isaiah,
traditionally taken to prophesy the Virgin Birth, '*Ecce, virgo peperit*' (Behold,
a virgin shall give birth).[70] There is also a correspondence between the three
gifts of the Magi to the infant Jesus and the constituents of the Stone.[71]

Any mention of stones in the Bible attracted alchemical exegesis. A popular and obviously attractive comparison was between the Stone of the Philosophers and the biblical stone rejected by the builders, first heard of in
Psalms, applied by Christ to himself and taken up by St Paul in the Epistles.
Jung's 'lapis-Christ' parallel is present in the fourteenth-century Lullian

72 Manget 1702: i 884.
73 *Truth's golden harrow*
in *Ambix* 3 (1949), cited
Coudert 1980: 96.

74 All the images in
Arnald of Villanova,
*Tractatus parabolicus* [ed
Seville, 1514, cf
Thorndike 1923–58 iii:
660] are of the Passion of
Christ, Halleux 1979: 85.

75 Helvetius 1670: 20.

*Codicil*,[72] and Robert Fludd talks of Christ the cornerstone.[73] The life of
Christ, his Passion and Resurrection, and also, but to a lesser degree, the life
of the Virgin, both found parallels in alchemy. In the emblem for cibation in
*Symbola aureae mensae* we see the Virgin suckling her child, and the accompanying chapter compares the birth of the Stone to the Nativity, sublimation
to the Passion, the black stage to Christ's death on Calvary and of course the
red stage to the Resurrection,[74] when the Stone is a crowned king, emerging
from his glassy sepulchre with a glorified body.[75]. The previously sceptical
Helvetius subsequently believed what he had seen and handled, as did

## LAPIS, VT INFANS, LACTE NVTRIENDVS
### est virginali.

 Elchior Cibinensis Vngarus, si populi tri-
bum spectemus in genere, alias Transsyl-
uanus habetur, vir Religiosus & Sacerdo-
tali ordini initiatus, vt verus artifex arca-
na huius scientiæ abditissimæ sub forma
sacra, nempe Missę, cõprehendit & adum-
brauit. Vidit enim hic vir doctus, quod Lapidi philosophi-
co attribueretur quasi Natiuitas, vita, sublimatio seu in i-
gne passio, atque hinc mors in nigro & tenebroso colore;
Denique resurrectio & vita in rubeo & perfectissimo co-
                                           Sſſ 3                 lore,

76 Helvetius 1667: 8–9.

77 W B 'The magistery'
in Ashmole 1652: 343.
78 Halleux 1979: 141.

doubting Thomas.[76] The alchemical King must enter again his virgin mother's womb.[77] The Transfiguration on Mount Tabor was allegorically interpreted,[78] and Nicholas Flamel found that the 'Book of Abraham the Jew' contained images of the Massacre of the Innocents.

79 Ashmole 1652: 263–4.

The pure King in 'The worke of John Dastin' works miracles on earth, clearing eyesight and making the lame walk, and later prays to his father to take away 'the Challice of hys passion' as Christ does in the Agony in Gethsemane.[79] The Assumption (and Coronation) of the Virgin were read as the glorification of matter. Such religious images offended the (ultra-Protestant?) iconoclast who defaced the *Rosarium* drawings in one Sloane manuscript.

Alchemy could even illuminate the mysteries of the Godhead and the Faith generally. Ripley in the 'Prologue' to the *Compound of alchymy* makes a

*Fig. 41 (opposite) The Virgin suckling the Child. 'The Stone, like a child, must be nourished with virgin milk'. Michael Maier,* Symbola aureae mensae *Frankfurt 1617).*

[BL, 90.i.25, 509]

*Fig. 42 (below, left and right) Defaced drawings of alchemical religious illustrations, the Coronation of the Virgin and the Resurrection, copied from the* Rosarium *series. These illustrations, like those in* PLATES XIV *and* XV, *draw on the series in* Rosarium philosophorum *(Frankfurt 1550)*

[BL, Sloane MS 299, ff.17–17v]

80 Read 1939: 110.

connection between the Stone and the mystery of the Godhead.[80] Von Lamb-sprinck portrays Trinitarian aspects of salt, sulphur and mercury and 'Bloomfield's blossoms' narrates a dream-vision of the Trinity, which illuminated the philosophers' sayings that the Stone was 'three in Substance, and one in Essence'.[81] It is difficult to know in the Epilogue to *Aureum seculum redivivum*[82] whether it is God or the Stone that is being praised, or indeed whether, in a sense, the author makes any distinction between them. George Ripley thought that sulphur was like the Holy Ghost as it was 'quick' and raised the body from death to life, presumably alluding to the Holy Spirit's description in the Creed as *vivificantem*.[83]

81 Ashmole 1652: 306.
*See also* the disquisition on the Trinity in *Aurora consurgens*, Aquinas 1966: 80ff, and also the 'Allegorical expressions betwixt the Holy Trinity and the Philosophers' Stone' in Basil Valentine, *Last will and testament*, Coudert 1980: 89.
82 *Musaeum Hermeticum* 1678: 70–2.
83 George Ripley, 'Mistery of alchymists' in Ashmole 1652: 383.
84 Halleux 1979: 141.
85 Ripley 1591: sig. FV.

Alchemy was like other aspects of the faith, especially its eschatology. The sixth-century theologian Aeneas of Gaza invoked alchemical ennobling of metals to demonstrate the transfiguration of resurrected bodies.[84] In the white stage the stone will be brought to Paradise after its pains in Purgatory.[85]

Paradox has been identified as one of the characteristic rhetorical figures of alchemy: its language also sometimes echoes the liturgy. Thomas Norton chose to call his alchemical work the *Ordinal* 'like as the Ordinalle to prestis settith owte / The servyce of the dayes'.[86] Sometimes mystical declarations of the nature of the Stone can sound like the Athanasian or Nicene Creed on the Second Person of the Trinity:

86 Norton 1975: line 129.

> It is a matter which the earth bringeth forth, and descends from heaven,
> waxeth pale and red, is born, is dead, riseth againe, and after liveth for ever.[87]

87 William Gratacolle in H P 1652: 68.

and there are echoes of the Creed's clauses declaring the Son's procession from the Father in phrases like '*argentum vivum de argento vivo, et sulphur de sulphure*'.

Since progress, growth, improvement and ennoblement are concepts constituting much alchemical thought, so its metaphors often draw on vegetable and human generation and growth. The germination of wheat was an analogy used by the early Greek texts (*see* Chapter 1, p.22), and similarly alchemists frequently quoted John 12:24–5 on the ear of wheat dying, and 1 Corinthians 15:36–8. 'The graine of Wheate which on the ground doth fall, / But it be dead it may not fructifie'.[88] The alchemical process was sometimes thought of in terms of an agricultural cycle: sowing, growth and harvesting. But if wheat grows from seed, then so do human beings,[89] and it is to human reproduction, conception, gestation, birth and indeed the subsequent life of man, that alchemical processes were more often compared.

88 'The worke of John Dastin' in Ashmole 1652: 259.
89 Stavenhagen 1974: 16.

> And so the stone, just like a man, is conceived from a mixture of two seeds, masculine and feminine, is transformed into an embryo through impregnation, is born into the light of day, is nourished with milk, grows, reaches maturity, is bound in marriage, breeds from his wife, is afflicted by a cross or by a tide of tribulations, dies, is buried, remains for some time in the grave, from there it arises, and enjoys new incorruptible life and is not able to die any more.[90]

90 *Symbola aureae mensae*, 510, cited Coudert 1980: 111.

*Fig. 43 Conjunctio sive Coitus. Rosarium philosophorum (Frankfurt 1550).*
[BL, 1032.c.1, sig. F3v]

# ROSARIVM

## CONIVNCTIO SIVE
### *Coitus.*

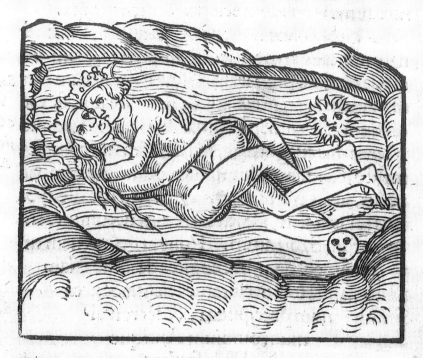

O Luna durch meyn vmbgeben/ vnd susse mynne/
Wirstu schön/ starck/ vnd gewaltig als ich byn·
O Sol/ du bist vber alle liecht zu erkennen/
So bedarsstu doch mein als der han der hennen.

## ARISLEVS IN VISIONE.

Coniunge ergo filium tuum Gabricum dile=
ctiorem tibi in omnibus filijs tuis cum sua sorore
Beya

Fig. 44 (above) Two stages of the alchemical operation as conception and pregnancy. Johann Daniel Mylius, Anatomia auri (Frankfurt 1628).
[BL, 1033.1.6, pars v, p. 8]

Fig. 45 (opposite) A chemical wedding. Vier Tractätlein Fr Basilii Valentini in Dyas Chemica (Frankfurt 1625).
[BL, 1034.h.21, p. 17]

As we have seen, all metals are generated (*procreantur*) of mercury and sulphur.[91] A sexual act was therefore necessary to produce the Stone, whose composition is like the generation of man. For the conduct of this operation you must have pairing, production of offspring, pregnancy, birth and so on,

> Marriage, increase, pregnancy, birth and nourishment are necessary to you in the conduct of this operation. For when conjunction has happened, conception follows, and pregnancy arises from conception, and birth follows pregnancy.[92]

The union of the principles had its social aspect in alchemical images of marriage and there are endless references to the marriage of the red man and the white woman, an idea attributed to Rasis by John Sawtre.[93] Chemical weddings of male sulphur and female mercury abound.[94]

Mercury was usually thought of as female and the mother of metals, and is referred to throughout the English alchemical poem 'Liber patris sap-

91 Bacon, *Speculum alchimiae* in Geber 1541: 258.

92 Stavenhagen 1974: 28.

93 H P 1652: 26; Cf Norton 1975: lines 2663–4, 'Then is the faire white woman / Mariede to the rodie man'.
94 Coudert 1980: 116.

THE LANGUAGES OF ALCHEMY

Um vierten / so nimb diß Aurum potabile , so von der helffte des purpurfarben Goldpulvers auß der Anima Solis gemacht worden/geuß es zu der solution Solis / so von der andern helffte des purpurfarben Goldpulvers gemacht worden / vnnd wiegs zusammen / vnnd gieß eben noch so viel des Ohls vom Victriol dazu / welches durch den Spiritum vini præpariret worden / alß dieses im Gewichte zusammen hat / vnnd addire allhier das Sal Solis darzu/thu es zusammen in ein newen Pellican / welcher in der grösse seyn solle / daß drey Theile davon im vndern Theile lehr bleiben / vnd der vierdte Theil aller erst mit der Materie erfüllet sey / sigillirs hermetice zu / vnd setze den Pellican in den Philosophischen Ofen / laß stehen darinnen / vnnd halte im Anfang das

ptimum

95 Ashmole 1652: 194–209.

96 'Mistery of alchymists' in Ashmole 1652: 381.

97 'Liber patris sapientiae' in Ashmole 1652: 199.
98 'Sir Edward Kelle's work' in Ashmole 1652: 326.

99 Sawtre in H P 1652: 27.
100 Rulandus 1612: 455; Albertus Magnus, *Compositum de compositis* quoted Crosland 1962: 18.
101 'Bloomfield's blossoms' in Ashmole 1652: 321.

102 Sawttre, in H P 1652: 31.

103 Ripley 1591: sig. E3.

104 Taylor 1948: lines 180–7.

105 Coudert 1980: 132–4.

106 'The worke of John Dastin' in Ashmole 1652: 266.
107 Artephius 1624: 212.

ientiae'[95] as 'she'. In a work by George Ripley, mercury is an unruly woman 'in her working . . . full wild' who has to be governed, and is not let out until she has conceived a child.[96] A fragment of a poem by Pearce, the Black Monk, describes the woman as 'both wanton and rude' presumably because of mercury's volatility. Alternatively mercury could be a good wife and mother, and although wooed by many would deal only with her husband;[97] or a wife who kills herself to bring life to her child.[98] Sulphur is the father of metals, the male active principle of Aristotelian physiology, and it is his seed, the Sperm of Sol, which should be cast into the matrix of mercury in copulation.[99] One of Rulandus' definitions of sulphur is as the 'seed' of the Stone, and 'Sulphur is as the father, mercury the mother of metals'.[100] Sex took place in the alchemical vessel, which in many texts is figured as a marriage bed. The red man and the white woman are put in a glass bed to die and regenerate.[101]

The metaphorical marriage bed was sometimes bizarre. John Sawtre quotes Senior's advice on (metaphorically) digging up a grave and laying the wife with her husband in the belly of the horse until they are conjoined – an allegory of the rather more mundane process of conjoining male and female principles (sulphur and mercury?) in a vessel gently warmed in horse dung.[102] A metaphorical conjunction of sex and death was more common. Helvetius describes the Stone at the end of the process as the King of the philosophers coming '*ex sui sepulchri vitrei thalamo*' (out of a tomb which is a glass bridal chamber). After the woman has conceived by the man, the matrix should be closed and the seed nourished with temperate heat.[103] As after conception the matrix closes, so that no foul matter can enter in, so the alchemist too should take care to close the alchemical vessel.[104]

Some unions and conceptions were more straightforward than others. Incest figures in some: in an emblem in Maier's, *Atalanta fugiens*, and in *Le triomphe hermetique*,[105] and in the vision of Arisleus of the incestuous union of Gabricus and Beya in the *Rosarium*. Sometimes the king conceives by his mother,[106] (*see* PLATE XVII) and sun and moon must enter their mother's womb to be born again.[107] There is a narrative of an exclusively male generation, conception and gestation in the book called *Lambspring*, where an old, ailing father almost dies without his absent young son and revives at his return, but in his eagerness swallows the son out of joy, and then lies in bed sweating and beseeching God to bring his son out of his body.

*Fig. 46 (opposite, above left) Mercury as a woman. Leonhardt Thurneisser zum Thurn,* Quinta essentia *(Munster 1570)*
[BL, 1032.c.10, sig. P4]

*Fig. 47 (opposite, above right) Man and wife unite in an alembic in a 16th century drawing.*
'The red man here to his white wyfe
Ys maryed with the spryte of lyfe'
[BL, Egerton MS 845 f.16]

*Fig. 48 (opposite, below)* Putrefactio. *The king and queen lie in their glass tomb.* Viridarium chymicum *figura LXVI, sig. S2]*

THE LANGUAGES OF ALCHEMY

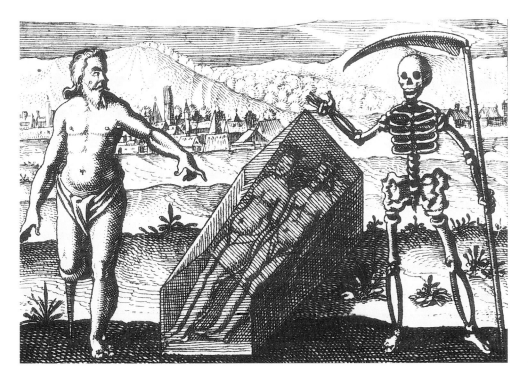

Conjunge fratrem cum sorore & propina illis poculum amoris:

## EPIGRAMMA IV.

NOn hominum foret in mundo nunc tanta propago,
    *Si fratri conjunx non data prima soror.*
*Ergo lubens conjunge duos ab utroque parente*
    *Progenitos, ut sint fœmina másque toro.*
*Præbibe nectareo Philothesia pocla liquore*
    *Utrisque, & fœtus spem generabit amor.*

                                      D             Lex

*Fig. 49 'Join the brother and the sister and offer them the loving cup'. Michael Maier,* Atalanta fugiens *(Oppenheim 1617).*
[BL, 90.i.19, Emblem IV, p. 25]

PLATE XIV *(previous page) A miniature from* Splendor
solis *showing a stage in the alchemical process which
draws on visual representations of the Baptism of Jesus.*
[BL, Harley MS 3469, f.21v]

PLATE XV *(above) The Coronation of the Virgin from 'The
Booke of the Rosary of philosophers' written by Lübeck in
1588.*
[BL, Additional MS 29,895, f.126v]

PLATE XVI (above) The Resurrection from 'The Booke of
the Rosary of philosophers': 'After my Passion and
manifould tormentes I am againe risen, beinge purified
and Clensed from all spottes'.

[BL, Additional MS 29,895, f.133v]

PLATE XVII (overleaf) The king crawls under his mother's
skirt to be re-conceived by her. From George Ripley,
Cantilena.

[George Ripley, Cantilena, Additional MS 11,388, f.36]

Me predatim penitus iuuentutis flore
Mors funasit sinditus xpe sed ab ore
Me audiui tertius grandi cum stupore
Renascendu de nuo nescio quo more

Regnu Dei aliter nequeo intrare
Hinc vt nascar denuo me humiliare
Volo matris fimibus meq reaptare
Nec non in materia prima discrepare

Ad hoc regem propria mater animauit
Eiusq conceptm se attestrauit
Quem statim sub clamude sua occultauit
Donec ipsum iterum ex se miarnauit

Mirum erat illico cernere conexum
Factum naturaliter, primu ad amplexu
Edere complacito ad ytrumq sexum
Per hiemis post aeris montana traduxerum

Mater tunc ingreditur thalamu pudoris
Sese sic in lectulo collocat honoris
Inter linthe amina plena q candoris
Signa statim edidit futuri langoris

Moribunda corporis virus emanabat
Quod materna faciem candidam sedabat
Hinc a se extraneos cunctos exterabat
Hostiuq camere stricte sigillabat

Vescebatur interim carnibus pauonis
Et bibebat sanguinem viridis leonis
Sibi quem Mercurius telo passionis
Ministrabat aureo cipho Babilonis

Impregnata igitur grauiter languebat
Certe nouem mensibus in quibus madebat
Visis autem lacrimis quas parturiebat
Lacte manens viridis Leo quod sugebat

Eiusq multicolor cutis apparebat
Nunc nigra nunc viridis nunc rubens fiebat
Seseq multociens sursum erigebat
Et post sese deorsum statim reponebat

Centu quinquaginta noctibus sic languebat
Et turbus totidem merus residebat
In triginta post modum rex ~~redolebat~~ reminiscebat
Cuius orto vermilo flore redolebat

The consequences of the union might be dangerous. During sex, Thabritius the philosopher (the male principle) was absorbed into the body of his wife Beya (*see* Chapter 2, Fig. 19).[108] In other accounts, the woman must be dead before the Stone appears. Aristotelian physiology considered women as imperfect or unfinished men, so the stage of the 'woman' either as mercury or the white elixir, is imperfect: there is too much wetness [moist humour] in a woman.[109] A more harmonious and stable state consequent upon union was often figured as a hermaphrodite, the alchemical 'Rebis'. Things could go wrong during conception and gestation. Albertus Magnus elaborates an image in which alchemical metaphors of the generation and conception of metals are combined with those of imperfect metals as diseased. Metals can become diseased in the earth,

108 Norton 1975: lxvi–lxvii.

109 Ripley, 'Mistery of alchemy' in Ashmole 1652: 385.

> just as a boy in his mother's belly contracts an infirmity from a corrupted womb because of an accident of place and through corruption, although the sperm was clean, yet the boy becomes leprous and unclean, because of the womb's corruption.[110]

110 Albertus Magnus in Gratarolus 1561: 80.

In 'The worke of John Dastin' the king's brothers are sick and scabby as their mother, mercury, conceived them in sin and fostered them with corrupt milk.[111]

111 Ashmole 1652: 260ff.

The foetus in the womb needed care, and the temperate heat needed to produce the white elixir was like gentle warmth of the womb. Care was needed too at the moment of birth (that is, at the accomplishment of the elixir), when the foetus needs the expulsive force of the womb or else dies.[112]

112 Petrus Bonus 1546: f.50.

*Fig. 50 (above, left and right) The father swallows his son and lies in bed sweating and waiting for his rebirth.* Lambspring *in* Dyas chemica *(Frankfurt 1625).*
*[BL, 1034.h.21, Emblems XIII and XIV, pp. 113 and 115]*

Rebis, ut Hermaphroditus, nascitur ex duobus montibus,
Mercurii & Veneris.

# EPIGRAMMA XXXVIII.

REm geminam REBIS veteres dixêre, quod uno
    Corpore sit mas hæc fœmináque, Androgyna.
Natus enim binis in montibus HERMAPHRODITUS
    Dicitur, Hermeti quem tulit alma Venus.
Ancipitem sexum ne spernas, nam tibi Regem
    Mas idem, muliérque una eadémque dabit.

              X               So-

113 Browne 1948: 22.

114 Bacon 1597: 10.

115 'Hunting of the
green lion' in Ashmole
1652: 286.

116 Ripley *Compound*
1591: sig. H2v.

The alchemical child needed attention and nutrition after its birth. Cleopatra compares philosophers contemplating their work to an affectionate mother contemplating and nourishing a child[113] (on the Stone as a child *see* Rulandus, *Lexicon* sv *filius*). Bacon compares the increase in heat needed in the alchemical process to feeding a child first with light, and then with stronger food when its bones have strengthened,[114] and Hortulanus in his commentary on the 'Emerald Table' recommends fermentation which he compares to nourishing the child. The child should be given drink,[115] but care should be taken not to feed it too much during the operation of cibation.[116]

Petrus Bonus was right when he said that the Stone could be compared by analogy with anything in the world. Alchemists shared some of their assumptions, terms and 'motifs idéologiques' with both medical practitioners and astrologers. All had assumed for several hundred years sympathies and symmetry between all created things, and, to quote the 'Emerald Table' again, 'That which is above is like to that which is below, and that which is below is like to that which is above, to accomplish the miracles of one thing'.

When William Gratacolle, translating Gratarolus, catalogues synonyms for the Stone, they appear to us as a most heterogeneous jumble, including gold, sun, brass of the philosophers, body of magnesia, rubine stone, kybrik, a man, green vitriol, tail of the dragon's milk, a dead body, water of sulphur, urine, the light of lights, marvellous father, fugitive servant, Brazil, chaos, dragon, serpent, toad, green lion, adder, poison, and, as Gratcolle honestly admits 'almost with other infinite names of pleasure'.[117]

117 H P 1652: 67–9.

Alchemy was adept at what seem to us unlikely comparisons. But alchemists inhabited a world where things were not only signified by their likes, but also by their opposites. It was a world where nothing was really unlike anything else.

*Fig. 51 The 'Rebis' or Hermaphrodite. Michael Maier,* Atalanta fugiens *(Oppenheim 1617).*
*[BL, 90.i.19, Emblem XXXVIII, p. 161]*

# CONCLUSION

The previous chapter was concerned with the languages of alchemy. It suggested that what distinguished alchemy from its offspring, chemistry, which begins to emerge as a separate science in the seventeenth century, was its language and the assumptions that language embodied. The condition of its language and the way that that language expressed its physics and metaphysics may be seen as constituting alchemy. From its earliest days those who wrote about alchemy constantly deployed intensely figurative and metaphorical language in their insistence on an internal unity and correspondence in the material world, and also on that world's unity, in turn, with the abstract and spiritual: sulphur, mercury and salt have a relationship, even as 'spirit and soul are in the body'.

Alchemy's characteristic mode of discourse is to express its truths in binary figures of language: paradox, enigma, equivocation and allegories which say one thing and mean another. Its characteristic choice of rhetorical tropes mimes its ideological belief in a universe in which matter itself is mysteriously instinct with life. And in alchemical thought and expression binary antitheses are complementary and exist only in the service of a final unity and completion: 'All are united in one which is divided into two parts', as Albert the Great's motto declares in Maier's *Symbola aureae mensae* (*see* Fig. 16). Hence the standard division of alchemical treatises into *theorica* and *practica*, the constant divisions and re-combinations of the work, the injuction *'solve et coagula'* (dissolve and then coagulate), fixing the volatile and making the fixed volatile, the circular ascents and descents of distillation, putrefaction and death which only spring into new life. Given this constant division only to unite, it is not really surprising that one of the alchemical stages most often discussed and represented is *conjunctio*.

Alchemy may be seen as articulating quite powerfully two myths cherished or longed for in western European culture: the unity of knowledge and the succession of knowledge. Even as alchemy stresses the unity of one work, one vessel and one Stone, so it flourished when the economy of knowledge and the arts was similarly unified. Its discourse assumes an organic unity of both knowledge and experience: there may be many books and opinions, but these were considered parts of one alchemical book that contained the plenitude of truth. '... though the Philosophers speak plurally / All is but one thing you may me well trowe', as George Ripley claimed. Or alchemical knowledge was often thought to be deliberately dispersed among many texts by the same master. One text provided fragmentary knowledge and only the whole corpus provided the full presence of truth. As it affirmed a unity of understanding, so alchemy insisted on an unbroken succession of knowledge, from Egypt to Greece, Greece to Islam, from adept to adept, book to book.

At the risk of a very large cultural generalisation, it is possible to detect change and fragmentation of this unity in the seventeenth century. In a century in England which saw the divisions of church and state, king and commons, king and parliament, so arts and sciences and branches of knowledge begin to go different ways and become distinct. The words *alchymia*

1 Halleux 1979: 47.

and *chymia* were 'rigorously synonymous'[1] until the seventeenth century, but not after that. The 'venture tripartite' of astrology, medicine and alchemy is no longer cohesive. The associations between the planets and the metals is noted in the third century when the theologian Origen described some Persian mysteries in which the soul was thought to ascend through the planetary spheres, passing through gates made of different metals, each associated with one of the planets: lead (Saturn), tin (Venus), bronze (Jupiter), iron (Mercury), an alloy (*'kerastou nomismatos'*) (Mars), silver (the

2 Origen 1857: column 1324.

Moon), gold (the Sun).[2] In the fourteenth century Chaucer's Canon's Yeoman can recite by rote the normal and commonplace analogies:

> Sol gold is, and Luna silver we threpe [assert],
> Mars iren, Mercurie quyksilver we clepe [call],
> Saturnus leed, and Juppiter is tyn,

3 'The canon's yeoman's tale', 826–9 in Chaucer 1957.

> And Venus coper, by my fader kyn![3]

It is a sign of the gradual change from alchemy to chemistry in the late seventeenth century when a text-book, Lemery's *Cours de Chymie* (1675) ridicules the supposed association between metals and the planets, altho gh the planetary names for metals continued to be used into the eighteenth

4 Crosland 1962: 80–1.

century,[4] as did many old alchemical symbols.

At the beginning of the seventeenth century, for John Donne alchemy was not only appropriate as a metaphor for a patron's wit ('To E. of D. with six holy sonnets'), but an image for the uncertainties and disappointments of love. Alchemical apparatus and technicalities are the analytical tools of the 'Nocturnall', where still 'plants, yea stones detest, / And love'. Donne could compare the risen Christ to the Elixir, and ask God the father alchemically to purge the soul from 'vicious tinctures'. Ben Jonson's play *The alchemist*, even though it apparently mocks the languages of alchemy, testifies to the syncretism of alchemical thought and writing: classical and Christian, religious and sexual. The Stone's most eager and well-informed seeker, Sir Epicure Mammon, is a man whose imagination and fantasies have alchemically amalgamated Christian and classical, the Bible and Ovid, Hercules and Solomon, and Roman Emperors with his own present.

The year 1660 saw the return of the king to England and his celebration in Dryden's 'Astraea Redux,' which tries to reassemble the fragments of royal charisma in a poem which both revives the *topos* of the return of the golden age and the old sympathetic analogies which alchemy, like other sciences, had assumed. In an aside in that poem, and in the year before the publication of Boyle's *The sceptical chymist*, Dryden's chimera of fancy 'Shuns the Mint like gold that Chymists make' – that is, it is unreal. In 1667 Milton's *Paradise Lost* was published, and in book III Satan visits the sun:

> The place he found beyond expression bright,
> Compared with aught on earth, metal or stone;
> Not all parts like, but all alike informed
> With radiant light, as glowing iron with fire;
> If metal, part seemed gold, part silver clear;
> If stone, carbuncle most or chrysolite,
> Ruby or topaz, to the twelve that shone
> In Aaron's breastplate, and a stone besides
> Imagined rather oft than elsewhere seen,
> That stone, or like to that which here below
> Philosophers in vain so long have sought,
> In vain, though by their powerful art they bind
> Volatile Hermes, and call up unbound
> In various shapes old Proteus from the sea,
> Drained through a limbeck to his native form.
> What wonder then if fields and regions here
> Breathe forth elixir pure, and rivers run
> Potable gold, when with one virtuous touch
> The arch-chemic sun so far from us remote
> Produces with terrestrial humour mixed
> Here in the dark so many precious things
> Of colour glorious and effect so rare?[5]

5 Milton, *Paradise Lost*
III 591–612.

At this specific moment in *Paradise Lost*'s narrative of creation, fall and recovery of a golden world, and at this moment in the seventeenth century, in 1667, we can hear a recapitulation of the history, theory and discourses of alchemy. The passage is dense in its reference: in its alchemical minerology, to the originally Aristotelian distinction between metals and stones, the pre-eminence of the two 'noble' and more 'perfect' metals gold and silver, perhaps also to the claims of some early Greek texts and Lullian alchemy to produce precious stones. Here too the appropriation and allegorization of biblical and classical authority by alchemical texts is displayed: some alchemical writers identified the *urim* in Aaron's breastplate with the Stone,

6 'He will bee gon, he
will evaporate. Deare
Mercury! Helpe! He
flies. He is 'scaped.
Precious golden
Mercury, be fixt; be not
so volatile'. Jonson,
*Mercury vindicated from
the alchemists at court*,
Jonson, *Works* 1925–52:
vii 409–10.

and alchemical exegesis read the classical myth of shape-shifting Proteus as the transformation of matter. Milton makes Hermes himself, the founding father of alchemy, take that place usually occupied by the notoriously 'volatile' Mercury[6] as the object of the alchemists' attention. There are the alchemical technicalities of words like 'volatile', the Greek-Arabic derivations in 'limbeck' and 'elixir', a glance at a heated medical-alchemical controversy over *aurum potabile* in early seventeenth-century England, and the overwhelming importance of the sun in alchemical thought and expression.

The text here, as is so often the case with *Paradise Lost*, is ambiguous in the way it voices natural philosophy, and Milton does not commit himself to anything too definite. The passage articulates a world-view that goes right back to the beginnings of alchemy, while simultaneously expressing sceptical reservations. The text will not finally reject imaginatively the possibility of a stone 'Imagined rather oft than elsewhere seen, / That stone, or like to that which here below / Philosophers in vain so long have sought'. The long search for the Philosphers' Stone is sceptically voiced in the reiteration of 'in vain . . . in vain', yet lingers on and continues: 'so long have sought' indicates a search that has not ceased. The passage is sceptical yet allows us a retrospect on the imaginative and epistemological coherence of the subject of its ironic treatment. The Stone's existence, if it does exist, is consigned to the fictional site of Milton's sun, not 'here below'. Like William Perkins' dream of the Philosophers' Stone, it seems now 'but a conceit, and no where to be found, but in *Utopia*.'

# GLOSSARY OF ALCHEMICAL TERMS

This glossary is limited to the most common alchemical ideas, processes, and substances, and serves largely to gloss alchemical terms that would otherwise have to be explained *seriatim* in the text of this book. I have not attempted to include alchemical synonyms. Those who want fuller glossaries should consult the concise and inclusive list given in Halleux 1979: 109–11. Terms given in bold within the glossary text have their own glossary entries.

**ablution** purification of bodies with suitable liquids; washing a solid with a liquid, usually water; **exaltation** by frequent infusions, and bringing back to purity.

**adustion** action or process of burning or scorching; inflammability, combustion.

**albation** whitening; *figured* as a swan.

**albification albation**.

**alchemy** from Arabic *al-kimia*, which is in turn from the Greek *chemeia* [?transmutation, defined by Suidas as the 'preparation of silver and gold']. In its turn *chemeia* may be derived from *Khem*, an ancient word for Egypt, and the word was perhaps later confused with Greek *chumeia* [infusion]; the transmutation of base metals into gold. 'Alchemy is a branch of knowledge by which the origins, causes, properties and passions of metals are thoroughly known, and by which those that are imperfect, unfinished, mixed and corrupt are changed into true gold' (Petrus Bonus 1546: f.26v); 'a science teaching the transformation of metals,

*Fig. 52 The alchemical king and queen in their bath.* Rosarium philosophorum *(Frankfurt 1550).*
[BL, 1032.c.1, sig. E2v.]

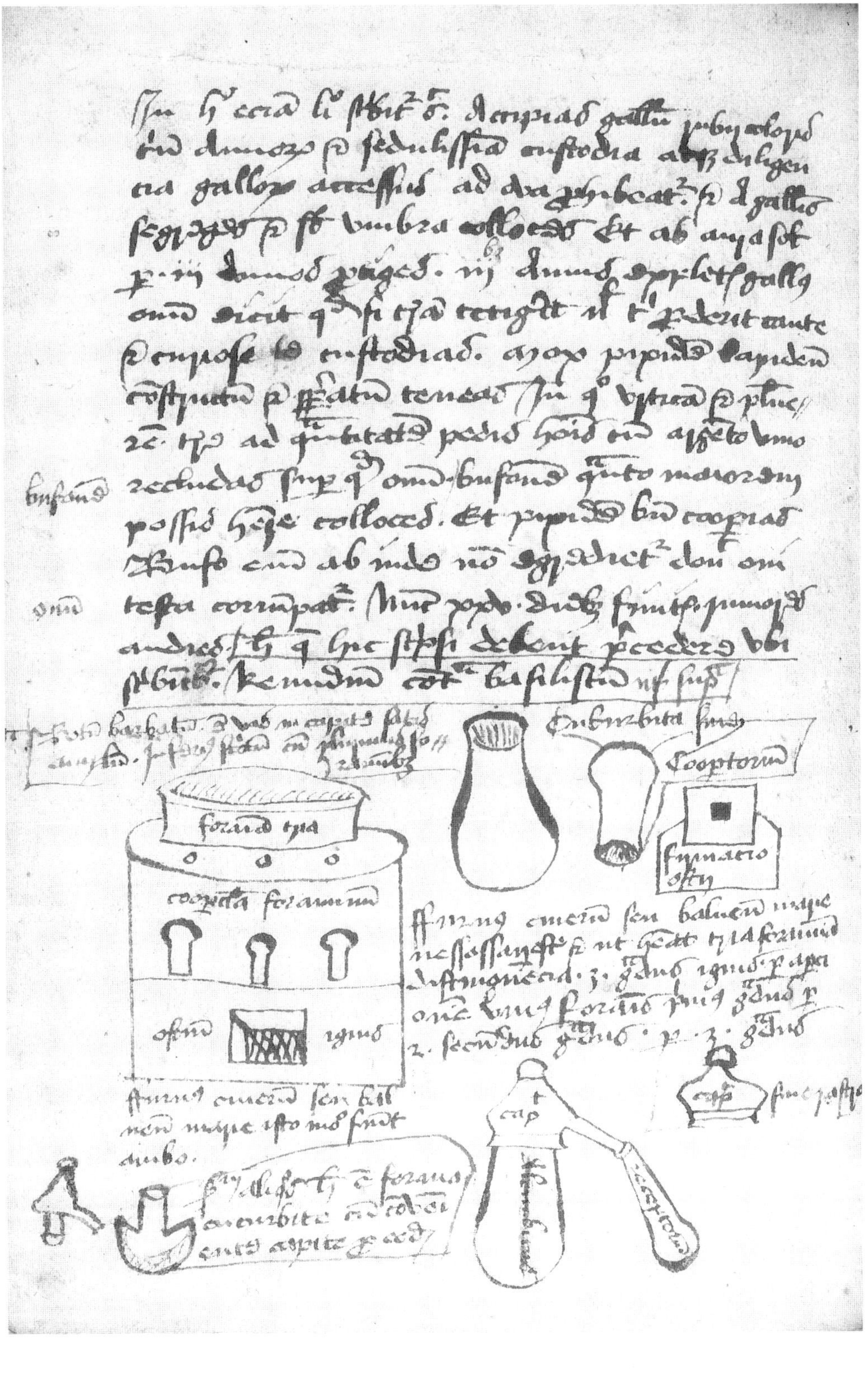

Fig. 53 (opposite) Drawing of a still. The parts are labelled caput (head) alembicus (alembic) and receptorium (receiver).
[BL, Sloane MS 1091 f.70v.]

Fig. 54 (left) A personification of 'Alchymia'. Leonhardt Thurneisser zum Thurn, Quinta essentia (Munster 1570).
[BL, 1032.c.10, sig. C3.]

Fig. 55 (above) The wolf devoured the king, and after it had been burned it restored the king to life'. Michael Maier, Atalanta fugiens (Oppenheim 1617).
[BL, 90.i.19, Emblem XXIV, p.105.]

which is effected by a medicine' (Bacon, *Speculum alchimiae* in Geber 1541: 258); 'the separation of the impure from a purer substance' (Rulandus 1612: 26); separation of the pure from impure (Dorn 1650: sig. Aaav).

**alcohol** from Arabic *al-kohl*, originally a metallic powder used to stain eyes, hence any fine powder, hence essence, hence quintessence, hence spirit of wine. Paracelsus speaks of the alcohol of wine; 'the purer and clearer part of a substance separated from the impure' (Rulandus 1612: 27).

**alembic** from Arabic *al-anbiq*, which is in turn from **ambix** [Greek: cup, beaker, or head of still]. Strictly speaking the upper part of a **still**, the still-head (also **limbeck**, **helm**, helmet), and hence used wrongly, and popularly, to mean the whole still. As a **still**, an apparatus used for **distillation** consisting of: a **cucurbit** containing the substance to be distilled, the alembic proper, ie the head or cap, whose beak conveyed vaporous products to a **receiver** in which they were condensed. The beak of the alembic was sometimes called 'the stag's horn'.

**alkali** from Arabic *al-qali* [plant-ashes]; originally a saline substance obtained from calcined ashes of marine plants; salt derived from ashes.

**aludel** from Arabic *al-uthal*; pear-shaped earthenware vessel or glass bottle open at both ends, used as a condensing receiver for the sublimates in **sublimation**.

**amalgamation** softening of metals by combination with mercury, hence combination of metals in an alloy.

**ambix** [Greek: cup or saucer] early technicians made mercury by heating cinnabar on an iron saucer; *see* **alembic**.

**antimony** a brittle metallic substance, the *stibium* of the ancients; a metal extracted from kohl or stibnite, or any metal or alloy resembling it; figured as *lupus metallorum* [the wolf of metals].

**aqua fortis** nitric acid, also used of other powerful solvents.

**aqua regia** [literally 'royal water'] a mixture of **aqua fortis** [nitric acid] and *spiritus salis* [hydrochloric acid] which has solvent action on the royal metal, gold.

# Das Büch zü Distilieren die züsa

men gethonen ding: Composita genant: durch die einzigen
ding/vñ das büch Thesaurus pauperum genant/für die armen yetz von neüwem wider ge=
truckt vnd von vnzalbarn irzthumen gereynigt vnnd gebessert/für alle voraußgangen truck/
etwan von Hieronimo Brunschwick außgeklaubt vnd geoffenbart zü trost vnd
heyl den menschen/nützlich yr leben darauß zü erlengern vnd yre
leib in gesundtheyt zü behalten.

Fig. 56 (opposite) The distillation of aqua vitae.
Hieronymus Braunschweig, Das Buch zu Distilliern
(Strassburg 1519).

[BL, 8904.l.3, title-page]

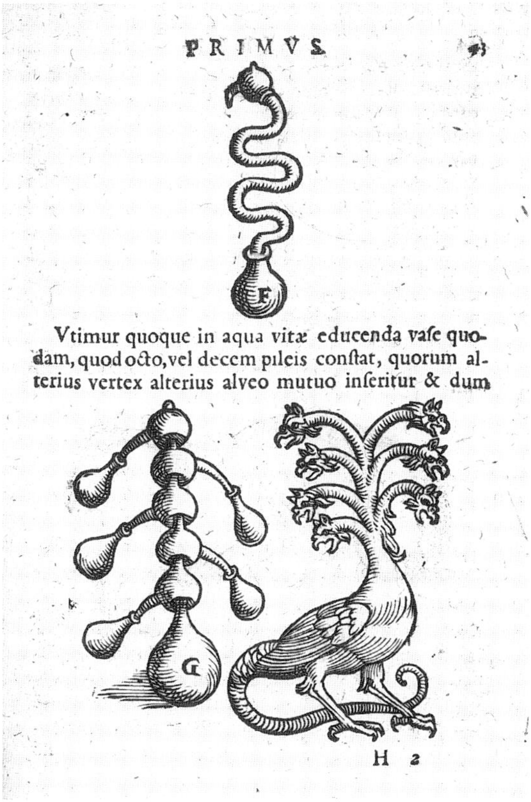

PRIMVS

Vtimur quoque in aqua vitæ educenda vafe quo-
dam, quod octo, vel decem pileis conftat, quorum alterius vertex alterius alveo mutuo inferitur & dum

Fig. 57 (right) Vases for distilling aqua vitae as a hydra.
Giovanni Baptista della Porta, De distillationibus libri
IX (Strassburg 1609).

[BL, 1037.1.15 (1), p. 43.]

H 2

**aqua vitae** aqueous alcohol concentrated by
distillation(s), ardent spirits, unrectified alcohol,
distilled wine.

**argent-vive mercury,** quicksilver.

**arsenic** from Greek: *arsenikon* [yellow **orpiment**];
arsenic sulphides, **realgar**, orpiment; *figured* as Luna,
our Venus, the companion of sulphur; 'Arsenicum is
the flashing of Metalls' (Dorn 1650: sig. Aaa4).

**ascension distillation,** evaporation.

**assation** roasting, baking; incinerating substances in
glass vessels to dry over ashes (Petrus Bonus 1894:
412).

**athanor** from Arabic *al-tannur*; digesting furnace used
by alchemists, in which constant heat was provided by
a tower which had a self-feeding supply of charcoal;
sometimes regarded as a furnace for incubation and
hence *figured* as the 'house of the chick'.

**atrament** a black substance; impure vitriol.

**auripigmentum orpiment**.

**azoth** from Arabic *al-zauq*; **mercury**, especially 'our

mercury' the hypothetical mercury supposed to be the
first principle of metals.

**balneum** a warming bath (of sand, water or ashes)
used in alchemical operations, particularly the water
bath *balneum Mariae* which took its name from its
supposed inventor, the early alchemist Maria
Prophetissa, which was used for separation and 'for the
performing the operations of that kind of moist
ascencions' (Dorn 1650: sig. Bbbv).

**bolt-head** round-bottomed flask with long neck, used
for distillation, especially of **aqua vitae**, also called
*matrass*; 'Did you look / O' the bolt's head yet?'
(Jonson 1991: II iii 35–6).

**borax** natural salt, including modern borax, but also
applied to other white minerals.

**calcination** reduction by fire of substances, usually
minerals, to powder or ash; subjection to roasting heat;
the word also covered other processes, such as the
addition of corrosive substances; 'pulvcrising of
substances by fire to remove the moisture uniting the
parts' (Albertus Magnus 1958: 412); pulverising over a
fire (Petrus Bonus 1894: 412); separation out of

Fig. 58 An athanor fed by its tower of charcoal; from the end of a 15th century MS of a commentary on an alchemical treatise, Tractatus in arte majori

[BL, Additional MS 10, 764 f. 109v.]

Fig. 59 The bath of the philosophers. Viridarium chymicum *(Frankfurt 1624)*

[BL, 717.d.63, Figura LXIV, sig. R4]

Fig. 60 A bolt-head, a vessel 'which we compare to ostriches, giraffes or cranes'. Giovanni Baptista della Porta, De distillationibus libri IX *(Strassburg 1609)*

[BL, 1037.1.15 (1)], p. 39.

Fig. 61 Calcination. Herbrandt Jamstahler, Viatorium spagyricum *(Frankfurt 1625)*

[BL, 1034.k.2 (1)], p. 200.]

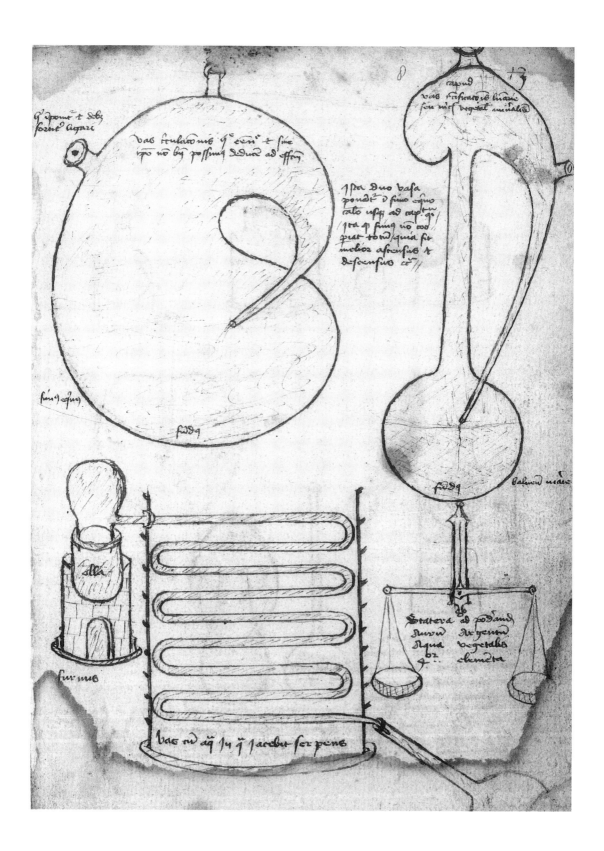

GLOSSARY OF ALCHEMICAL TERMS

moisture (Rulandus 1612: 125–6). 'Calcination is a treasure of a thing: do not weary of calcination' (Geber, *Liber fornacum* in Geber 1545: 185). When a substance was heated in an open or closed vessel, the oxidisation left a black substance *figured* as death, mortification, putrefaction, a tomb, coffin, crows and ravens, skulls, scenes of death and killing, **caput mortuum**.

**calx** product of **calcination**; after the matter has been put in an **urinal** and left on a great fire for a week, the product is ashes or 'philosophers' earth' (Raudorff in H P 1652: 59).

**calx vive** quicklime.

**caput mortuum** faeces left after distillation and sublimation.

**cement** (noun) a pasty mixture placed over sheets of metal to be heated in the furnace with a view to an examination of their purity; penetrating mineral substance as either powder or paste (Rulandus 1612: 137); (verb) to place substances in alternate layers.

**ceration** reducing hard substances to wax-like state, mollification, softening, sometimes to allow penetration by other substances; saturating substance with liquid (Petrus Bonus 1894: 411).

**ceruse** white lead.

**cibation** 'feeding the matter' see also **cohobation** and **imbibition** (*see* Chapter 4, fig. 41).

**cinefaction** reduction to ashes.

**cineritium cupel.**

**cinnabar** ore of mercury, mercuric sulphide.

**circulation** continuous distillation of liquid for the purpose of refining it, reflux distillation; **exaltation** of pure liquid by heat through **solution**, and **coagulation** in a **pelican**: it contains in itself the processes of **digestion**, **sublimation** and **distillation** (Rulandus 1612: 155).

**circulatory** closed glass vessel or double vessel allowing reflux **distillation** to take place; **pelican**

**coagulation** conversion of liquid to solid; solidification, either by crystallization or by the cooling of a fused substance; 'reduction of liquid substances to a solid mass by deprivation of their vapours' (Albertus Magnus 1958: 43); condensation and reduction to a solid state (Rulandus 1612: 157–8); 'the making of a thin thing thick' (Dorn 1650: sig. Bbb4v); *coagulum* is the key of the sages and is male and female joined together in one body (Petrus Bonus 1894: 279–80).

**cohobation** pouring back liquid distillate to its residue or faeces, followed by further distillation; **imbibition** of the medicine with its oil, *figures* as feeding the child.

**comminution** reduction of matter into minute parts by grinding or pounding.

**congelation** conversion of liquid to solid state, crystallization; a process whereby matter becomes thick, no longer flows and stands 'like ice on water' (Rulandus 1612: 167).

**conjunction** mixture or union of elements or substances *figured* as marriage, copulation, uniting of male and female or brother and sister or king and queen sometimes to form an androgyne; the moment of conception (*see* Chapter 4, figs 43, 44, 45, 49, 51).

**copperas** sulphates of iron, copper or zinc.

**crocus, crocus of iron, crocus martis** ferric oxide.

**crosslet crucible.**

*Fig. 63 Congelation. Herbrandt Jamstahler,* Viatorium spagyricum *(Frankfurt 1625)*
*[BL, 1034.k.2 (1), p. 203.]*

*Fig. 62 (opposite) Vessels for circulation*
*[BL, Sloane MS 338, f.8.]*

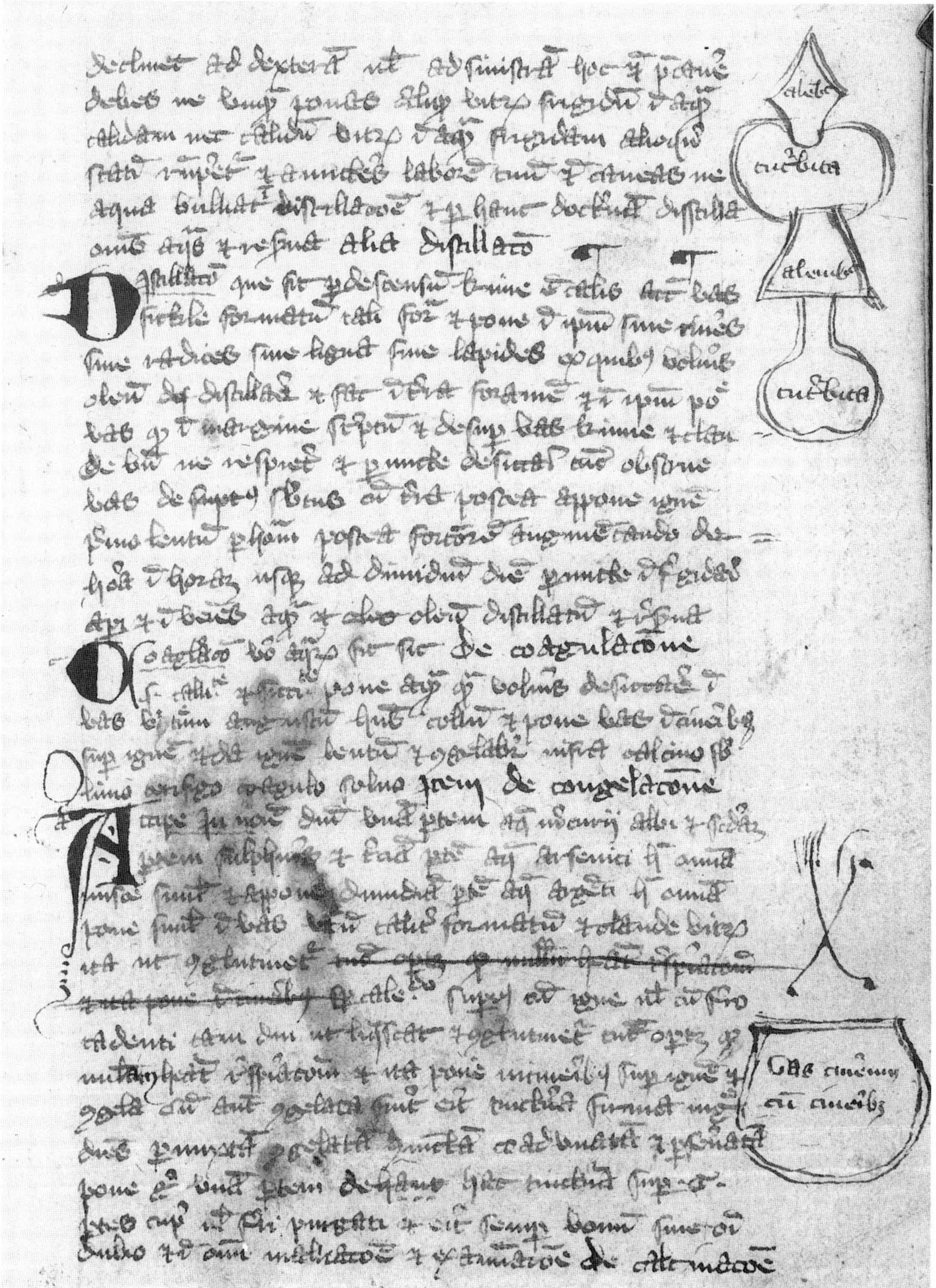

**crucible** vessel which can withstand great heat, used for melting and liquefying metals: it has a narrow base widening into a round or triangular body. In this vessel the final alchemical process of **projection** or transmutation usually took place.

**cucurbit(e)** [Latin: gourd] gourd-shaped vessel which was the lower part of a **still**, made of earthenware or glass, containing the original liquid to be distilled; 'a vessel for the most part cone-shaped in the shape of a gourd or pear, swelling like a womb' (Rulandus 1612: 178).

**cupel** shallow cup made of bone-ash or other porous material, often used for refining, testing or assaying gold or silver.

**cupellation** heating in **cupel** in a current of air for the purpose of refining.

**dealbation albation**.

**descension** a method of distillation or fusion in which fire is applied on top of the vessel and the liquid product or **essence** flows down into the **receiver** below; reduction of metallic calx to metal in which the fused metal flowed down into a receiver at a lower level.

**descensory** chemical furnace in which liquid falls downward from the gross matter.

**digestion** maturation, preparation of a substance with gentle heat modelled on the process by which food was thought to be digested in the stomach; separation of pure from impure.

**dissolution** separation into parts or constituent elements, disintegration, decomposition; *see also* **solution**.

**distillation** there were three main kinds: by **ascension, descension** or filtration; the rising of vapours of a liquid in its own container such as an **alembic** or a process in a **descensory**, but in both cases the purpose is purification (Albertus Magnus 1958: 46):
(a) conversion by means of a **still** into vapour by means of heat and then condensation by cooling, extraction of spirit or essence, separation of the volatile from the fixed; purification of water drop by drop, by

*Fig. 64 An alembic on top of a cucurbit from a manuscript of Albert,* Semita recta.
*[BL, Sloane MS 323 f. 77.]*

*Fig. 65 Different methods of distillation Geber,* Alchemiae Gebri Arabis *(Berne 1545)*
*[BL, 1607/963], p. 188.]*

conversion into steam and then condensing (Petrus Bonus 1894: 414); a process 'by which the essence is extracted in the form of a liquid, and is brought condensed in a dropping moisture, transferred from the vessel containing the matter into the receiver placed below' (Rulandus 1612: 183); **ascension**; *figured* as vapours ascending from earth to heaven, a tail-eating serpent, flight of birds.
(b) **descension**.
(c) sometimes applied to the removal of one liquid to another by capillary movement through a wick or strip of cloth; could also include what we would now call filtration.

**elements** the four Aristotelian principles of matter· fire, earth, air and water; an element according to Paracelsus 'is the corruptible and transient essence of the world, and of all things which are subject to change' (Dorn 1650: sig. Ccc2v).

**elevation** vaporisation by means of heat; a process in which spiritual portions are elevated from the corporeal, the subtle raised from the gross in the form of vapour at the top of the vessel; dry elevation is **sublimation**, humid elevation is **distillation** (Rulandus 1612: 195–6).

**elixir** from Arabic *al-iksir*, in turn from Greek: *xerion* (powder for wounds); the medicine, the agent of transmutation, the philosopher's stone; an 'incomparable medicine', a ferment which will amalgamate with a mass of material having affinity with itself (Rulandus 1612: 197).

**essence** extract, tincture, indispensable quality, extract obtained by **distillation**, a fine extract continuing the nature and perfection of the substance from which it is derived.

**exaltation** the **elevation** of a substance to a higher dignity and virtue, augmentation in intensity 'I exalt our med'cine / By hanging him in *balneo vaporoso*' (Jonson 1991: II iii 102–3).

**fermentation** an idea of the process of transmutation in which the Stone worked on other substances like yeast, converting them to gold, or a stage in the alchemical process in which the Stone converts mercury into itself; *see* **multiplication**; *figured* as leavening bread with yeast; gold is the ferment of the elixir, without which the philosophers' medicine cannot be perfected and is as leaven to dough or as curd to milk for cheese. The ferment of gold is gold (John Dastin, quoted by Holmyard 1957: 147).

**filtration** 'straining a thing through a woollen cloth or paper' (Dorn 1650: sig. Ccc3v).

**fixation** depriving substance of its volatility, fluidity or mobility; turning spirit to body (Raudorff in H P 1652: 56–7); operation on a **volatile** subject after which it is no longer volatile, but remains permanent in the fire, which is performed by calcination or slow decoction (Rulandus 1612: 215); 'making a thing which flies the fire to endure the fire' (Dorn 1650: sig. Ccc3v).

**fixed** the state of a substance after **fixation**; *figured* as dragons or lions without wings.

**gripe's-egg** griffin's egg, vessel of Hermes.

**helm** upper part or head of still, **alembic**.

**horse-dung** being usually at a higher temperature than surrounding objects, was employed to give a gentle but protracted heat; *equi clibanum, equi ventrum*.

**imbibition** soaking or saturation with liquid, **cohobation**.

**inceration** ceration.

**ingression** cohobation.

Fig. 66 *Fermentation*. Viridarium chymicum *(Frankfurt 1624)*

[BL, 717.d.63.], figura XLVI, sig. N2.

Fig. 67 *Fermentation*. Rosarium philosophorum *(Frankfurt 1550)*

[BL, 1032.c.1, sig. O2.]

**inhumation** placing soluble substance in animal dung (sometimes mixed with pigeon dung and vinegar) for **dissolution** (Petrus Bonus 1894: 414); burying in earth, **putrefaction** (Rulandus 1612: 267–8).

**kerotakis** [Greek: literally, artist's palette?], reflux apparatus for treating metals with vapours: the process was said to involve continual blackening, whitening and yellowing.

GLOSSARY OF ALCHEMICAL TERMS

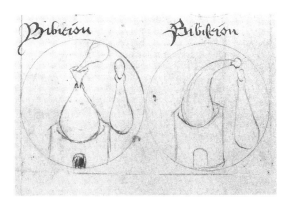

Fig. 68 'Bibicion'.
[BL, Harley MS 2407 f. 108.]

**magisterium, magistery** [literally, quality of mastery] the master principle of matter, transmuting agency, the medicine, the philosopher's stone; exalted matter (Rulandus 1612: 310); cf the title of Geber's treatise *Summa perfectionis magiserii*.

**magnesia** vague term for several mineral substances, which included manganese dioxide and magnetite, as well as our present magnesia; *figured* as the whitening snow, the bridal procession, the stainless chiton (Coudert 1980: 66).

**marcasite, marchasite, markasits** pyrites; imperfect metallic substance 'of as many species as there are solid metals' (Rulandus 1612: 318).

**mercury** one of the principles of metals; 'is mentioned everywhere, in every alchemical work, and is supposed to perform everything' (Rulandus 1893: 229); *figured* as 'he who imbibes glass as a thirsty man cold water, joining of sun and moon, the electrum of nature, and is called the fugitive slave' (Petrus Bonus 1894: 202); 'the cloud of clouds, the father enriching the son, eye of wisdom, the pregnant woman that conceives and brings forth in the same day' (extract from Rasis, *Lumen luminum* in Bonus 15467: f. 171), water of life (Ripley in Ashmole 1652: 394).

**merds** excreta.

**minium** red lead.

**mollification** softening.

**multiplication** commonly synonymous with transmutation, but strictly a concentration of the

Fig. 69 Two Mercuries. *'Give fire to fire, mercury to mercury and that will be enough for you'*. Michael Maier, Atalanta fugiens *(Oppenheim 1617)*
[BL, 90.i.19 Emblem X, p. 49.]

Fig. 70 Multiplication. Viridarium chymicum *(Frankfurt 1624)*
[BL, 717.d.63, Figura XLVIII, sig. N4.]

**lac virginis** [Latin: the virgin's milk] a liquid 'wherein they say Metalls are dissolved' (Dorn 1650: sig. Aaa); also known as the philosophers' vinegar, mercurial water, sophic water, the dragon's tail, mercury of the philosophers.

**lute** [Latin: mud] cement used in sealing apertures and joints of apparatus.

Stone's transmuting power or an increase in the amount of the Stone; *figured* as saffron spreading its colour.

**orpiment** from *auripigmentum* [golden pigment]; bright yellow metallic substance that glitters with golden colours; yellow sulphide of arsenic; early alchemists throught it contained gold; its Greek name is confusingly *arsenikon*.

**pelican** circulatory **still** with two side-arms; 'a circulatory vessel, given its name through its likeness in shape to a pelican piercing its breast with its beak and stuffing its chicks full, with a full belly gradually narrowing to a more slender neck which, twisting and curving back, the mouth directs the flow to the belly' (Rulandus 1612: 360).

**phial** small glass bottle, 'a glass vessel like a sphere with a round belly which sends out a slender funnel, frequently used in **coagulation** and **solution**' (Rulandus 1612: 361).

*Fig. 71 A pelican. Giovanni Baptista della Porta,* De distillationibus libri IX *(Strassburg 1609)*
*[BL, 1037.1.15 (1)], p. 41.]*

*Fig. 72 Putrefaction. Herbrandt Jamstahler,* Viatorium spagyricum *(Frankfurt 1625)*
*[BL, 1034.k.2 (1)], p. 38.]*

**prima materia**, **prime matter** 'the philosophers have given this many names and almost every possible description for they didn't know how sufficiently to praise it' (Rulandus 1612: 322–3); Rulandus gives 50 and Waite ádded another 84 (Rulandus 1892: 223–5).

**principles** following Paracelsus, the three or 'hypostatical' principles of the alchemists were sulphur, mercury and salt.

**projection** the final alchemical process, throwing the powder or Stone upon the molten metal to be transmuted, thus changing it to gold or silver; addition of the elixir to the metal whose transmutation was desired; **exaltation** of a substance by the medicine: it differs from **fermentation** in that it instantly transforms by 'a sudden entry' (Rulandus 1612: 384).

**putrefaction** disintegration or decomposition of a substance, conversion of metal into apparently inert mass or powder; *figured* as the crow's head, crow's bill, ashes of Hermes' tree, toad of the earth, mortification, death of grain of wheat, slaying of bodies, hell, Cimmerian darkness.

**quintessence** essential and most refined part of a substance, 'a certaine spirituall matter extracted corporeally out of hearbs, plants, and all things that have life, and the exalting of it to the highest degree of purity, by separating all impurities' (Dorn 1650: sig. Eee4).

**realgar** [Arabic] red sulphide of arsenic.

**receiver** vessel for receiving the product of **distillation**.

**retort** glass vessel with long neck, globular vessel with a small neck issuing from the body and gradually bent round into an oblong pipe.

**rubification** reddening.

**sal ammoniac**, **sal armoniac** ammonium chloride, natural and artificial, used in washing, purifying and cleansing processes; *figured* as an eagle.

**salt** common salt; Albert said it was the key to the art, opens and closes all things and no alchemical work can be completed without it (Albertus Magnus 1958: 27).

**sandarach orpiment**.

**sandifer** dross from molten metal.

**separation** dividing into members, division of the pure from the impure (Raudorff in HP 1652: 53) *figured* as raising the birds from their nest.

*Fig. 73 Retort as a stork. Giovanni Baptista della Porta, De distillationibus libri IX (Strassburg 1609).*
*[BL, 1037.1.15 (1)], p. 44.]*

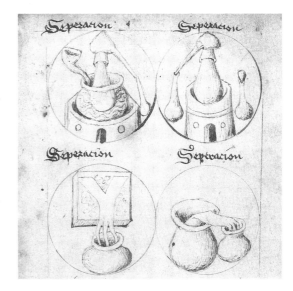

*Fig. 74 Methods of 'Seperacion'.*
*[BL, Harley MS 2407 f. 107.]*

*Fig. 75 Separation. Viridarium chymicum (Frankfurt 1624).*
*[BL, 717.d.63, Figura XXXIX, sig. L3.]*

**solution** turning solid to liquid, dissolving solid in liquid; turning the dry into wet (Raudorff in H P 1652: 52); the resolution of any calcined substance into water (Albertus Magnus 1958: 45); reduction of calcined body to water (Petrus Bonus 1894: 413).

**spirit** a volatile substance which sublimes on heating, eg **sal ammoniac**.

**spirits** so called because they allow elevation and escape the fire (Rulandus 1612: 442); according to the alchemists they were seven in number: four principal and three minor, although the lists differ: **sulphur**, **mercury**, **orpiment** and **sal ammoniac** were the principal spirits and three minor, **marcasite**, **tutia** and **magnesia**; or mercury, sulphur, orpiment or arsenicum, and sal ammoniac (Albertus Magnus 1958: 18); mercury, sulphur, orpiment, sal ammoniac, and marcasite, magnesia, tutia (Petrus Bonus 1894: 60); mercury, sulphur, sal ammoniac and arsenic (Rasis, Partington 1938: 192, Vincent of Beauvais, cited

Thorndike ii 471–2 and Gower, *Confessio* in Ashmole 1652: 368–9); mercury, sulphur, arsenic, sal ammoniac, and tutia, magnesia, marchasite (pseudo-Aristotle, *De perfecto magisterio* in Crosland 1962: 6); Rasis numbered four spirits and Geber seven which includes these four (Crosland 1962: 13); mercury, sulphur, orpiment, sal ammoniac and marcasite, bismuth, and tutia (Rulandus 1612: 442); 'The firste spirit quyksilver called is, / The seconde orpyment, the thridde, ywis, / Sal armonyak, and the ferthe brymstoon.' (Chaucer, 'Canon's yeoman's tale', Chaucer 1957: lines 822–4).

**still** apparatus for **distillation**, sometimes called **alembic**; it has three parts: the body or vessel in which the material is heated, the still head, which is the cool part for condensing vapour and the **receiver**.

*Fig. 76 Sublimation. Herbrandt Jamstahler,* Viatorium spagyricum *(Frankfurt 1625).*
*[BL, 1034.k.2 (1), p. 213.]*

GLOSSARY OF ALCHEMICAL TERMS

*Fig. 77 Urinal, also called* ursale *(a bear). Giovanni Baptista della Porta,* De distillationibus libri IX *(Strassburg 1609).*
[BL, 1037.1.15 (1), p. 40.]

**sublimation** conversion of solid to vapour, followed by condensation of the vapour in solid form upon cool surface; 'the volatilizing of a dry substance by fire, causing it to cling to the sides of the vessel' (Albertus Magnus 1958: 40); in sublimation we have a soul rising towards heaven (Bonus 1546: f. 38v); *figured* as angels.

**sulphur** one of the two principles of metals; 'our sulphur' is 'nothing other than the fatness of the earth, made thick by temperate cooking, until it becomes hard and dry' (Rulandus 1612: 453); *figured* as the shadow of the sun, coagulum of quicksilver, vinegar of the sages, golden tree (Petrus Bonus 1894; 238); ordinary sulphur was one of the **spirits** of alchemy and was *figured* as a dog.

**tincture** a colouring liquid, hence the **elixir**, the philosophers' stone.

**tutia**, **tutits**, **tutty** from Arabic *tutiya*, zinc carbonate or oxide.

**urinal** glass vessel.

**usifur** from Arabic *zanjifar*, **cinnabar**.

**vessel** the receptacle in which the **elixir** was made; *figured* as sieve, dung, furnace, sphere, green lion, prison, house of the chicken, chamber, philosopher's egg, bed, tomb.

**vitriall** glistening crystalline body.

**vitriol of Cyprus** copper sulphate.

**volatile** literally 'flying', a natural substance with a tendency to vaporise and fly upwards; *figured* as dragons or lions with wings, birds flying upwards; its alchemical opposite is **fixed**.

**white arsenic** arsenious oxide.

**white water** mercury.

# BIBLIOGRAPHY

Albertus Magnus 1890–9: Albertus Magnus, *B. Alberti Magni . . . Opera omnia* ed Augustus Borgnet 38 vols (Paris 1890–9)

Albertus Magnus 1958: [pseudo-] Albertus Magnus, *Libellus de alchimia ascribed to Albertus Magnus* tr Sr Virginia Heines (University of California Press: Berkeley and Los Angeles 1958)

Aquinas 1561: Thomas Aquinas *S. Thomae Aquinatis . . . in libros meteorologicorum Aristotelis praeclarissima commentaria* (Venice, 1561)

Aquinas 1966: Marie-Louise von Franz, *Aurora consurgens: A document attributed to Thomas Aquinas* ed with a commentary by Marie-Louise von Franz (Bollingen series, Pantheon Books: NY 1966)

Artephius 1624: Artephius, *Artephius his secret booke* (1624)

Ashmole 1652: Elias Ashmole, *Theatrum chemicum Britannicum* (1652)

*Auriferae Artis* 1572: *Auriferae artis, quam chemiam vocant, antiquissimi authores, sive Turba Philosophorum. In hoc primo volumine continentur . . .* (Basle 1572)

Avicenna 1927: [pseudo-] Avicenna, *Avicennae De congelatione et conglutinatione lapidum* Latin and Arabic texts with an English tr, ed E J Holmyard and D C Mandeville (Paul Guenthner: Paris 1927)

Bacon 1859: Roger Bacon, *Opera quaedam hactenus inedita* ed J S Brewer (Rolls series, 1859)

Bacon 1597: [pseudo-] Roger Bacon, *The mirror of alchimy* [tr of *Speculum alchimiae*] (1597)

Francis Bacon 1627: Francis Bacon, *Sylva sylvarum or a naturall history* (1627)

Berthelot 1885: Marcellin Berthelot, *Les origines de l'alchimie* (Paris 1885)

Berthelot 1888: Marcellin Berthelot, *Collection des anciens alchimistes grecs* (3 vols Paris 1888)

Berthelot 1893: Marcellin Berthelot, *La chimie au Moyen Âge* (3 vols, Paris 1893)

Petrus Bonus 1546: Petrus Bonus, *Pretiosa margarita novella* ed Janus Lacinius Calabrus (Venice 1546)

Browne 1948: C A Browne, 'Rhetorical and religious aspects of Greek alchemy' *Ambix* 3 (1948), 15–25

Caley 1926: Earle Radcliffe Caley, 'The Leyden papyrus X' *Journal of chemical education* 3 (1926) 1149–66

Chaucer 1957: Geoffrey Chaucer, *Works* ed F N Robinson, 2nd ed (Oxford University Press: London 1957)

Coudert 1980: Alison Coudert, *Alchemy: the philosopher's stone* (Wildwood House: London 1980).

Crosland 1962: Maurice P Crosland, *Historical studies in the language of chemistry* (Heineman: London and Toronto 1962)

Debus 1962: Allen G Debus, 'An Elizabethan history of medical chemistry' *Annals of science* 18 (1962), 1–29

Debus 1965: Allen G Debus, *The English Paracelsians* (Oldbourne: London 1965)

Debus 'Significance' 1965: Allen G Debus, 'The significance of the history of early chemistry' *Cahiers d'histoire mondiale* 9 (1965) 39–58

Donne 1952: John Donne, *The divine poems* ed Helen Gardner (Clarendon Press: Oxford 1952)

Donne 1965: John Donne, *The elegies and the songs and sonnets* ed Helen Gardner (Clarendon Press: Oxford 1965)

Dorn 1650: Gerard Dorn, *A chymicall dictionary explaining hard places and words met withall in the writings of Paracelsus, and other obscure authours* tr J[ohn] F[rench] (1650)

Duncan *MLN* 1942: Edgar Hill Duncan, 'Chaucer and "Arnold of the Newe Toune"' *Modern language notes* 57 (1942) 31–3

Duncan 1942: Edgar Hill Duncan 'The alchemy in Jonson's *Mercury vindicated* '*Studies in philology* 39 (1942) 625–37

Eliade 1962: Mircea Eliade, *The Forge and the Crucible* tr Stephen Corrin (2nd ed University of Chicago Press: Chicago and London, 1962)

Ferguson 1915: John Ferguson, 'The Marrow of Alchemy' *Journal of the alchemical society* 3 (1915) 106–29

Flamel 1624: *Nicholas Flammel, his exposition of the Hieroglyphicall figures which he caused to bee painted upon an arch in St Innocents church-yard, in Paris* tr Eirenaeus Orandus (1642) [tr of Nicholas Flamel *Les figures hieroglyphiques de Nicolas Flamel* 1612]

Fobes 1915: F H Fobes, 'Medieval Versions of Aristotle's *Meteorology*' *Classical philology* 10 (1915) 297–314

Geber 1541: Geber [ie pseudo-Jabir ibn Hayyan], *In hoc volumine De alchemia continentur haec...* (Nuremberg 1541)

Geber 1545: Geber [ie pseudo-Jabir ibn Hayyan], *Alchemiae Gebri Arabis philosophi solertissimi, Libri* [contains *De investigatione, Summa perfectionis, De inventione veritatis, De fornacibus construendi* and alchemical texts by other authors] (Berne 1545)

Geber 1928: [ie pseudo-Jabir ibn Hayyan], tr Richard Russell, *The works of Geber Englished by Richard Russell, 1678* a new ed with intro E J Holmyard (Dent: London and Toronto 1928)

Geber 1991: Geber [ie pseudo-Jabir ibn Hayyan], [*Summa perfectionis magisterii*] *The Summa Perfectionis of pseudo-Geber*, a critical edition, translation and study by William R Newman (Collection de travaux de l'Academie internationale d'histoires des sciences, vol 35, E J Brill: Leiden, NY, Copenhagen, Cologne 1991)

Ginzburg 1990: Carlo Ginzburg, *Myths, emblems, clues* (Hutchinson Radius: London, 1990)

Gratarolus 1561: Gulielmus Gratarolus, *Verae alchemiae artisque metallicae, citra aenigmata* (Basle 1561)

Halleux 1979: Robert Halleux, *Les textes alchimiques* Typologies des sources des moyen âge occidental (Brepols: Turnhout 1979)

van Helmont 1707: Johann Baptista van Helmont, *Opera omnia* (Frankfurt 1707)

Helvetius 1667: John Frederick Helvetius, *Johannis Friderici Helveti Vitulus aureus, quem mundus adorat & orat* (Amsterdam 1667)

Helvetius 1670: John Fredrick Helvetius, translated William Cooper, *The golden calf which the world adores and desires* (1670) [tr of *Johannis Friderici Helveti Vitulus aureus, quem mundus adorat & orat*]

Holmyard 1957: E J Holmyard, *Alchemy* (Penguin: Harmondsworth 1957)

Hopkins 1967: Arthur John Hopkins, *Alchemy, child of Greek philosophy* (AMS Press: New York 1967, repr of Columbia University Press: New York 1934)

Hunter 1983: Michael Hunter, *Elias Ashmole 1617–1692. The founder of the Ashmolean Museum and his world. A tercentenary exhibition.* (Ashmolean Museum: Oxford 1983)

Jonson, *Works* 1925–52: *Ben Jonson* ed C H Herford and Percy and Evelyn Simpson (11 vols Clarendon Press: Oxford 1925–1952)

Jonson 1991: Ben Jonson, *The alchemist* ed Elizabeth Cook, New Mermaids, (A&C Black: London 1991)

Josten 1949: C H Josten, 'William Backhouse of Swallowfield' *Ambix* 4 (1949) 1–33

Jung *Works* 1953–79: C G Jung, *Collected works* tr R F C Hull 20 vols (Routledge 1953–79)

Kibre 1940: Pearl Kibre, 'The *Alkimia minor* ascribed to Albertus Magnus' *Isis* 32 (1940) 267–300

Kibre 1942: Pearl Kibre, 'Alchemical writings ascribed to Albertus Magnus' *Speculum* 17 (1942) 499–518

Kibre 1944: Pearl Kibre, 'An alchemical tract attributed to Albertus Magnus' *Isis* 35 (1944) 303–16

Kibre 1954: Pearl Kibre, The *'De occultis naturae* attributed to Albertus Magnus' *Osiris* 11 (1954) 23–39

Kibre 1958: Pearl Kibre, 'Albertus Magnus, *De occultis nature' Osiris* 13 (1958) 157–83

Kibre 1959: Pearl Kibre, 'Further manuscripts containing alchemical tracts attributed to Albertus Magnus' *Speculum* 34 (1959) 238–47

Kibre 1980: Pearl Kibre, 'Albertus Magnus on alchemy' in ed James A Weishepl, *Albertus Magnus and the sciences: commemorative essays* (Pontifical Institute of Medieval Studies: Toronto 1980), 187–202

van Lennep 1985: Jacques van Lennep, *Alchimie: contribution à l'histoire de l'art alchimique* (2nd edition Brussels 1985)

Little 1914: ed A G Little, *Roger Bacon essays: contributed by various writers on the occasion of the commemoration of the seventh centenary of his birth* (Clarendon Press: Oxford 1914)

Lowes 1913: J L Lowes, 'The dragon and his brother' *Modern language notes* 28 (1913) 229

Manget 1702: J J Manget, *Bibliotheca chemica curiosa* 2 vols (Cologne 1702)

Molland 1974: A G Molland, 'Roger Bacon as magician' *Traditio* 30 (1974) 445–60

Montgomery 1963: John Warwick Montgomery, 'Cross, constellation and crucible: Lutheran astrology and alchemy in the age of the Reformation' *Transactions of the Royal Society of Canada* 1, series 4 (June 1963) 251–70 [also published in *Ambix* 11 (1963) 65–86]

*Musaeum Hermeticum* 1678: *Musaeum Hermeticum reformatum et amplificatum, omnes Sopho-Spagyricae artis discipulos. . . continens tractatus chimicos XXI* 2nd ed enlarged, (Frankfurt 1678 [first ed 1625])

*Musaeum Hermeticum* tr Waite 1893: tr A E Waite, *The hermetic museum restored and enlarged* 2 vols (1893)

Nierenstein 1932: M Nierenstein and P F Chapman, 'Enquiry into the authorship of the *Ordinall' Isis* 18 (1932) 290–321

Nierenstein 1934: M Nierenstein and F M Price, 'The identity of the manuscript entitled Mr Nortons worke' *Isis* 21 (1934) 52–6

Norton 1975: Norton, Thomas, *Ordinal of alchemy* ed John Reidy, Early English Text Society (Oxford University Press: London, New York, Toronto 1975)

Origen, *Contra Celsum* in J P Migne, *Patrologia, Cursus Completus* Series Graeca, tom xi (Paris 1857)

H P 1652: *Five treatises of the Philosophers Stone. . . by the paines and care of H. P.* 1652 [containing:
[1] Two of Alphonso King of Portugal
[2] One of John Sawtre a Monke
[3] Another written by Florianus Raudorff, a German philosopher
[4] Also a treatise of the names of the Philosophers Stone, by William Gratacolle, translated into English
[5] To which is added the Smaragdine Table]

Patai 1983: Raphael Patai, 'Biblical figures as alchemists' *Hebrew Union College annual* 54 (1983) 195–229

Partington 1937: J R Partington, 'Albertus Magnus on alchemy' *Ambix* 1 (1937), 3–20

Partington 1938: J R Partington, 'The chemistry of Razi' *Ambix* 1 (1938) 192–6

Pereira 1989: Michela Pereira *The alchemical corpus attributed to Raymond Lull* Warburg Institute Surveys and Texts XVIII (Warburg Institute: London 1989).

Plessner 1954: Martin Plessner, 'The place of the *Turba philosophorum* in the development of alchemy' *Isis* 45 (1954) 331–8

Read 1939: John Hinton, *Prelude to chemistry* 1936, 2nd ed 1939

Reidy 1957: John Reidy 'Thomas Norton and the *Ordinall of alchimy' Ambix* 6 (1957), 59–85

Ripley 1591: George Ripley, *The compound of alchymy* (1591)

de Rola 1973: Stanislaus Klossowski de Rola, *The secret art of alchemy* (Thames and Hudson: London 1973)

Rossi 1961: Paolo Rossi, 'The legacy of Ramon Lull in 16th century thought' *Medieval and Renaissance studies* 5 (1961) 182–213

Rulandus 1612: Martin Rulandus, *Lexicon alchemiae sive dictionarium alchemisticum* (Frankfurt 1612)

Rulandus 1892: A E Waite, *A lexicon of alchemy* [tr of *Lexicon alchemiae sive dictionarium alchemisticum*] (1892)

Ruska 1935: Rasis [ie Muhammad ibn Zakariya Al-Razi][*De aluminibus et salibus*], *Das Buch der Alaune und Salze* ed Julius Ruska, (Berlin 1935)

Sandys 1970: George Sandys, *Ovid's Metamorphosis Englished, mythologized and represented in figures* ed Karl K Hulley and Stanley T Vandersall (University of Nebraska Press: Lincoln, Nebraska)

Sarton 1927–48: George Sarton, *Introduction to the history of science* 5 vols (Baltimore 1927–48)

Sheppard 1959: H J Sheppard, 'The redemption theme and Hellenistic alchemy' *Ambix* 7 (1959) 42–6

Singer 1928: Dorothea Waley Singer, 'The alchemical *Testament* attributed to Raymund Lull' *Archeion* 9 (1928) 43–52

Singer 1932: Dorothea Waley Singer, 'Alchemical writings attributed to Roger Bacon' *Speculum* 7 (1932) 80–6

Stavenhagen 1974: ['Morienus', *Book of the composition*], ed and tr L Stavenhagen, *A testament of alchemy, being the revelations of Morienus . . . to Khalid ibn Yazid* (Brandeis University Press, University Press of New England: Hanover, New Hampshire 1974)

Steele 1929: Robert Steele, 'Practical chemistry in the twelfth century: Rasis, *De aluminibus et salibus*' *Isis* 12 (1929) 10–46

Suidas 1928–38: *Suidae lexicon* ed Ada Adler 5 vols (Teubner: Stuttgart 1928–38)

Taylor, 'George Ripley's song' 1946: F Sherwood Taylor, 'George Ripley's song' *Ambix* 2 (1946) 177–81

Taylor 1946: F Sherwood Taylor, 'Thomas Charnock' *Ambix* 2 (1946) 148–76

Taylor 1948: F Sherwood Taylor 'The argument of Morien and Merlin: an English alchemical poem' *Chymia* 1 (1948) 23–35

Taylor 1951: F Sherwood Taylor, *The alchemists: founders of modern chemistry* (Heinemann: London 1951).

Thorndike 1923–58: Lynn Thorndike *A history of magic and experimental science* 8 vols (Columbia University Press: New York 1923–58)

Lynn Thorndike and Pearl Kibre, *Catalogue of incipits of medieval scientific writings in Latin* (revised and augmented ed, Medieval Academy of America: printed London 1963)

*Turba* ed Ruska 1931: ed Julius Ruska, *Turba philosophorum: Ein Beitrag zur Geschichte der Alchemie* (Quellen und Studien zur Geschichte der Naturwissenschaften und der Medizin, Berlin 1931) [an ed of the Latin text with German tr and introduction]

*Turba* tr Waite 1896: *The Turba philosophorum, or assembly of the sages* tr A E Waite (G Redway: London 1896)

Vincent of Beauvais 1624: Vincent of Beauvais, *Speculum naturale* (Douai 1624)

Yates 1954: Frances Yates, 'The art of Ramon Lull: an approach to it through Lull's theory of the elements' *Journal of the Warburg and Courtauld Institutes* 17 (1954) 115–73

Yates 1960: Frances Yates, 'Ramon Lull and John Scotus Erigena' *Journal of the Warburg and Courtauld Institutes* 23 (1960) 1–44

# APPENDIX
# ALCHEMICAL TEXTS
# AND WRITERS: MANUSCRIPTS IN
# THE BRITISH LIBRARY

*Manuscripts in the British Library attributed to some of the alchemical authors in Chapter II.*

This appendix lists some BL MSS ascribed to some alchemists in this chapter, with the notable exceptions of Lull and Ripley. This is for reasons of space. For Lull, *see* the very full bibliography of MSS in Pereira 1989: 63–107. The British Library's MSS of Ripley are too numerous to list in a general book of this size and require a study of their own, which, as far as I know, has not yet been attempted.

The title of each work is given where possible, and the characteristic incipit or incipits are cited (words in brackets indicate variants in these incipits), together with the page numbers of the incipits in Lynn Thorndike and Pearl Kibre, *A catalogue of incipits of medieval scientific writings in Latin* (revised and augmented ed., Medieval Academy of America: London 1963) (TK). Also provided, where possible, is the number given to each work in Dorothy Waley Singer, *Catalogue of Latin and vernacular alchemical manuscripts in Great Britain and Ireland dating from before the 16th century* (3 vols Brussels 1928–31) (DWS).

This list does not claim to be exhaustive. It was compiled largely by consulting Singer's *Catalogue* and catalogues in the Manuscripts Students' Room at The British Library. It concentrates on the best-known works attributed to the authors in Chapter II.

## Albertus Magnus

*Alchimia*
incipit: 'Calistenus [Calixtenes] unus de antiquioribus' (TK 184), (DWS 180)

Sloane MS 3120, ff.174–192v: 'Incipit Tractatus Albertus qui sic incipit: Calixtenus unus philosophus', missing most of the first chapter, 16th cent., in Latin
Sloane MS 3457, ff.46–56v: 15th cent., in Latin (DWS 180)

*Compositum de compositis*
incipit: 'Talentum mihi traditum negotiationis domini non abscondam' (TK 1555)
Sloane MS 3630, ff.70–74v: 'Albertus Magnus, upon the worke or Science of Alchimie, named Compositum de compositis', 17th cent., in English

*Compositum de compositis* (extracts)
Sloane MS 276, f.3: 'Ex Alberto magno de compositi composito', 16th cent., in Latin
Sloane MS 3180, ff.12–13: 'Here begineth the draught of Albertus Magnus upon the worke or science of Alchimie named Compositum de Compositis', copied out by Edward Dekyngston, 17th cent., in English
Sloane MS 3684, ff.37–41: 'Here begineth the draught of Albertus Magnus, upon the worke, or science of Alchimie named, Compositum de Compositis', 17th cent., in English

*De occultis naturae*
incipit: 'In mutue allocutionis tractatu rogasti me' (TK 693), (DWS 182)
Arundel MS 164, ff.127–131: 'Albertus Magnus de occultis nature', 15th cent., in Latin, written in 1422 by a scribe in his 34th year (*see* f.131), (DWS 182)

*Semita recta*
incipit: 'Omnis sapientia a domino deo est' (TK 1002), (DWS 177)

**Harley MS 3542, ff.17–25v:** lacking the beginning, 14th cent., in Latin (DWS 177 vi)

**Sloane MS 316, ff.8–54:** 'Semita recta Alberti Magni', 16th cent., in English

**Sloane MS 317, ff.88–91v:** 'Semeta Recta', written *c*.1600, 17th cent., in Latin

**Sloane MS 323, ff.61v–84v:** 14th cent., in Latin (DWS 177 ii)

**Sloane MS 513, ff.168v–178:** ends f.168, 'Explicit semita recta alkemye Alberti', 14th cent., in Latin (DWS 177 vii)

**Sloane MS 633, ff.124–138:** 'Here begin the three Bookes of the workes of Alchymie, with their Chapters all here following: Authore Rogero Bacon [*sic*]', but f.138, 'Explicit Semita secundum Albertum in Alkymia', 16th cent., in English

**Sloane MS 830, ff.1–43v:** 'In Christi Namen: Amen. Hebt sich ann Die Großte Kunst Der Alchimey Alberti Theotonici. M A B 20 Aprilis 1575. Vorrede, Alle Weißheit unnd Kunnst kombe vo(n) Gott dem Herrn . . .'. The opening is a German version of the characteristic incipit of the *Semita recta*. 16th cent., in German

*The mirror of lights*
(This is part of the *Semita recta* and ends in the same way)

**Harley MS 3542, ff.1–14:** incipit f.1, 'In sechyng owte of the sothenes of the crafte . . .', 14th cent., in English

**Harley MS 3542, ff.35–41v:** explicit f.41v, 'Here endit the myrror of lyghtenys', 14th cent., in Latin

**Sloane MS 513, ff.155–168:** incipit f.155 'In schechyng owt the sothenes of this craft . . .' but explicit f.168, 'Expliti semita recta Alkymye Alberti', 15th cent., in English (DWS 183 iii)

*Semita recta* (excerpts)
**Sloane MS 299, ff.23–42v.** 'Ex Semita Alberti magni et Medulla Ripleyii', formerly belonging to Gabriel Gostwick, 16th cent., in English

**Sloane MS 317, f.99:** 'The translation into Englishe of some of the workes of Semeta Recta', written *c*.1600, 17th cent., in English

**Sloane MS 2128, ff.1–13v:** extracts in English and Latin, once in the possession of John Dee who annotated it and whose signature is on f.1 'Joannes Dee 1557', 15th cent., in Latin and in English (DWS 177 xviii)

**Sloane MS 3180, ff.1–11v:** 'Ex Semita Alberti Magni et Medulla Ripley' in English

**Sloane MS 3684, ff.1–36:** 'Ex Semita Alberti Magni et Medulla Ripleyii' 17th cent., in English

**Sloane MS 3744, ff.117v–124:** 'Notabilia Alberti Magni', 15th cent., in Latin (DWS 177 viii)

*Other works*
**Sloane MS 976, f.32v:** 'Compendium alberti super artem alkimie'. This is part of Albert's genuine work *De mineralibus* [*see* Kibre 1942: 506], 15th cent., in Latin (DWS 176 xiv)

**Sloane MS 323, ff.2–61v:** 'Hic incipit practica fratris alberti in alchimiam Que ab eodem dicitur Secretorum secretorum', 15th cent., in Latin (DWS 179)

# Roger Bacon

*Breve breviarium*
incipit: 'Breve breviarium breviter abbreviatum sufficit' (TK 180), (DWS 191)

**Sloane MS 276, ff.4–10v:** 'Incipit liber fratris Rogerii bachonis de naturis metallorum et ipsorum transmutacione potest eciam dici Incipit breve breviarium aliter breviloquium alkimie', 15th cent., in Latin (DWS 191 v)

*Epistola de secretis operibus* or *Epistola de potestate artis et naturae*
incipit: 'Vestre petitioni respondeo diligenter [quemadmodum] nam licet' (TK 1691), (DWS 190)

**Harley MS 3528, ff.1–3:** imperfect, lacking the beginning, 15th cent., in Latin (DWS 190 iv)

**Sloane MS 2156, ff.111–116v:** 'Incipit Epistola Rogeri Bachon de potestate artis et naturae', 15th cent., in Latin (DWS 190 v)

*Epistolae tres ad Johannem Parisiensem* or *Tractatus trium verborum*
incipit *Epistola I* or the whole *Tractatus trium verborum*: 'Cum ego Rogerus rogatus a pluribus sapientibus' (TK 296), (DWS 192)
incipit *Epistola II*: 'Cum promisi tibi mittere duas cedulas subsequentes' (TK 332), (DWS 192)
incipit *Epistola III*: 'Cum de ponderibus utilis sit distinctio' (TK 290), (DWS 192)

**Cotton MS Julius D V, ff.160–164:** [*Epistolae I* and *II*] and ff.152–158 [*Epistola III*]. The explicits (ff.161v, 164, and 158) are in a simple code, 14th cent., in Latin (DWS 192 i)

**Harley MS 3528, ff.81v–82v:** [*Epistola I*] 'Incipit tractatus Rogeri Bacon'; 'Secunda Epistola Rogeri bacon' ff.85–87 [*Epistola II*], ff.104–7 [part of *Epistola III*], 15th cent., in Latin (DWS 192 v)

Sloane MS 1091, ff.178–198: incipit 'Rogerus bacon Johanni Parisiensi salutem . . .', 15th cent., in Latin (DWS 192 vi)

Sloane MS 1754, ff.62–75: 'Mendacium primum Rogeri', the explicits at the end of all three letters (ff.63, 65, 75) are in code, 14th cent., in Latin (DWS 192 ii)

Sloane MS 2327, ff.25–26v: 'Incipit unum opus fratris rogeri Bacun' [Epistolae I and II]; ff.30v–33 [part of Epistola III], 15th cent., in Latin (DWS 192 vii)

Sloane MS 2327, ff.35–35v: 'Incipit liber avicennae de diverso modo ignium' is a fragment of Epistola III, as John Dee noted in the margin (f.35 'Bachonis fragmentum'), 15th cent., in Latin (DWS 192 viii)

Speculum alchimiae (in seven chapters). This work is also attributed to Simon of Cologne
incipit of the preface 'Multifarium [Multipharie] multisque modis loquebantur olim' (TK 888), (DWS 194)
incipit of the work 'In antiquis philosophorum libris satis' (TK 664), (DWS 194)

Additional MS 15,549, ff.101–110: 'Istum tractatum iam perfecte et breviter completum . . . super speculum alkemie'; ends (f.110),' . . . Amen. Anno domini. 1494. D. R. Et sic explicit liber qui vocatur Speculum alkemie de transmutacione metallorum.' 15th cent., in Latin (DWS 194 iv)

Harley MS 3528, ff.69–75v: 'Multipharie', 15th cent., in Latin (DWS 194 v)

Sloane MS 692, ff.1–9v: 15th cent., in Latin (DWS 194 vi)

Sloane MS 1118, ff.50–56v: 'Opus philosophicum', 15th cent., in Latin (DWS 194 vii)

Sloane MS 2325, ff.44–46v: (unfinished), 15th cent., in Latin (DWS 194 ix)

Sloane MS 2327, ff.36–38: (imperfect), annotated by John Dee, 15th cent., in Latin, (DWS 194 x)

Sloane MS 2405, ff.39–47v: 'The mirrour of alchimie composed by y$^e$ famous fryer Roger Bachon. sometime fellow of martin [sic, ie Merton] colledge and brasen nose colledge in oxenforde'; without the preface and the text diverges from the usual one after the first three chapters, 17th cent., in English

Sloane MS 3506, ff.42–46v: 'The Speculum Alchimiae of Roger Bacon', 18th cent., in English

Sloane MS 3744, ff.60v–64v: 'Multifarie multisque modis', 15th cent., in Latin (DWS 194 xi)

Speculum alchimiae (a different work from the Speculum in seven chapters above) incipits: 'Ad laudem et honorem summe et individue (TK 52), (DWS 196); or

'Salutem [quam] tibi [sibi] amice karissme' (TK 1370), (DWS 196); or 'Speculum alcimie qui in corde meo figuravi' (TK 1521), (DWS 196)

Harley MS 3528, ff.87–89v: 'Speculum Alchimae R: B.', 15th cent., in Latin (DWS 196 i)

Sloane MS 692, ff.114–116v: 'Incipit tractatus sciencie . . . Speculum Alchemiae', 15th cent., in Latin (DWS 196 ii)

Sloane MS 1118, ff.96–99: 15th cent., in Latin (DWS 196 iii)

Stowe MS 1070, ff.20–22: 'Incipit tractatus Rogeri Baconis', 15th cent., in Latin (DWS 196 iv)

Speculum secretorum alchemiae
incipit of prologue 'Ad instructionem [et doctrinam] multorum [tractantium] in hac arte [circa hanc nobilem artem] studere (TK 47), (DWS 197)
incipit of cap 1 'Scire igitur oportet te lector in principio' (TK 1406)

Additional MS 10,764, ff.154–155v: 15th cent., in Latin (DWS 197 vii)

Sloane MS 513, ff.178v–181v: 15th cent., in Latin (DWS 197 viii)

Sloane MS 1754, ff.48–50: 14th cent., in Latin (DWS 197 ii)

Other works attributed to Bacon
Verbum abbreviatum ed. Raymund Gaufridi, incipit: 'Verbum abbreviatum verissimum et approbatum' (TK 1688), (DWS 193)

Harley MS 3542, ff.28v–31: 15th cent., in Latin. (DWS 193 ii)

Sloane MS 1842, ff.32–36: 'Verbum abbreviatum Rogeri Baconis', incipit, 'Verbum abbreviatum verissimum et approbatum' is Raymund Gaufridi, Verbum abbreviatum de leone virdi (TK 1688), (DWS 193), 17th cent., in Latin

Sloane MS 288, ff.167–168v: 'Verbum abreviatum seu hortus Thesaurorum Rogeri Baconis' is not the Verbum abbreviatum

Other works
Harley MS 3528, ff.119–121v: 'Bacon', incipit 'Accipe lapidem benedictum' is extracts from an edn of the Secretum secretorum of Aristotle to Alexander attributed to Bacon; 15th cent., in Latin (TK 20) DWS 31)

Sloane MS 288, ff.136–138v: 'De Chemia, Rogerus Bacon etc', 16th cent., in Latin

Sloane MS 1118, ff.94–99: 'Speculum Alkamie' is part of Bacon's Opus minus, 15th cent., in Latin (DWS 187 iii)

Sloane MS 830, ff.52–78: 'Die Alchimistische kunst' in 32 chapters, written 10 May 1575 by 'M B', 16th cent., in German

Sloane MS 1799, ff.31–73v: 'Radix Mundi Rogeri Baconis Translated into Englishe by Robert Frelove. 1550', 16th cent., in English

Sloane MS 513, ff.184–188v: recipes in Latin and French, f.188v 'Explicit semita recta alkemie secundum magistrum Rogerum Bakun', 15th cent., in Latin and French (DWS 1113 vii)

## Arnald of Villanova

*Compositio lapidis . . . ex solo mercurio*
incipit: 'Quia plures philosophi scripserunt lapidem ex una re fieri' (TK 1228), (DWS 240)
Sloane MS 3457, ff.105v–109: 15th cent., in Latin

*Epistola super alchemia ad regem Neapolitanum*
incipit: 'Scias O tu rex quod sapientes posuerunt' (TK 1387)
Sloane MS 1068, ff.270–271v: (imperfect), 17th cent., in Latin
Sloane MS 3117, ff.85–94v: 17th cent., in Latin

*Epistola de sanguine humano ad magistrum Jacobum de Toledo*
incipit: 'Magister Iacobe amice [mi] carissime dudum me rogastis' (TK 842), (DWS 230)
Additional MS 27,584, ff.83–85: 'Epistola Magistri Arnaldi de catalonia ad Magistrum Jacobum de tholeto,' 15th cent., in Latin (DWS 230 i)
Sloane MS 75, ff.183v–184: 15th cent., in Latin (DWS 230 ii)

*Flos florum*
incipit: 'Vidi senem unum clarificatum [in una claritate]' (TK 1696), (DWS 227)
Stowe MS 1070, ff.40–41: 'De anulo' (DWS 227 ii)

*Medicina Hermetis cap V*
incipit: 'Hic incipit preparacio medicine' (TK 620), (DWS 241)
Harley MS 3542, ff.57–57v: 15th cent., in Latin

*Perfectum magisterium*
incipit: 'Scias carissime [fili] quod in omne re' (TK 1385)
Sloane MS 3086, ff.69v–75: 'Incipit perfectum magisterium & gaudium magnum, Arnoldi de villanova', 17th cent., in Latin

*Nota quod Magister Arnaldus de Villa Nova dedit . . . Magistro hospitalis Sancti Johannis*
incipit: 'In nomine domini amen. Recipe salis calcinatis' (TK 1334), (DWS 224 ii)
Sloane MS 976, f.28v: 15th cent., in Latin (DWS 225 ii)

*Novum lumen*
Prologue incipit: 'Pater et domine reverende licet liberalium artium' (TK 1029), (and see DWS 326)
Sloane MS 1068, ff.263–269: 17th cent., in Latin
A version of or commentary on *Novum lumen*
Incipit: 'In tractatu qui vocatur Rosarius philosophorum' (TK 719), (DWS 232)
Sloane MS 1091, ff.162–164: 15th cent., in Latin (DWS 232 iii)

*De perfectione operis alkimie* or *De secretis naturae* or *Thesaurus secretus operacionum naturalium*
incipit: 'Scito fili quod in hoc libro loquor' (TK 1407), (DWS 229)
Harley MS 3528, ff.93v–98: 'Dialogus inter magistrem et discipulum', 15th cent., in Latin (DWS 229 iv)
Sloane MS 692, ff.67v–74v: 15th cent., in Latin (DWS 229 v)
Sloane MS 1118, ff.89–92v: Glosa Arnoldi de Villa nova', 15th cent., in Latin (DWS 229 vi)
Sloane MS 1118, ff.115–122: 'Glosa Arnoldi de Villa nova', 15th cent., in Latin (DWS 229 vii)
Sloane MS 2327, ff.2–4v: 15th cent., in Latin (DWS 229 viii)

*Quaestiones tam essentiales quam accidentales*
incipit: 'Primo queritur si composito [operatio] lapidis potest fieri' (TK 1110), (DWS 235)
Additional MS 10,764, ff.66–71: 15th cent., in Latin
Sloane MS 3506, ff.1–32: 'Here Begin The Essential as wel as the accidental Questions of Arnold De Villa nova to Pope Boneface the Eight' 18th cent., in English

*Rosa novella in arte majori*
incipit: 'Non negligas homo ergo nobilissime hoc arcanum' (TK 921), (DWS 237)
Additional MS 10,764, ff.167v–168v: 'Incipit Rosa novella Magistri Arnaldi de villa nova in arte majori' 15th cent., in Latin

*Rosarius philosophorum* (This is probably by John Dastin and is attributed to both Dastin and Arnold in manuscripts)
incipit: 'Desiderable desiderium impreciabile pretium' (TK 403), (DWS 231)
Additional MS 10,764, ff.3–22v: 'Incipit opus

magistri Johannis Hastiri', 15th cent., in Latin (DWS 231 x)

**Additional MS 15,549, ff.122–133:** the date 1474 is on f.133, 15th cent., in Latin (DWS 231 xi)

**Harley MS 1818, ff.1–32v:** the name 'Robart Clarke' is on f.32v, 15th cent., in Latin (DWS 231 xii)

**Harley MS 2407, ff.49–50v:** 'Incipit tractatus qui vocatur Rosarius' 15th cent., in Latin (DWS 231 xiii)

**Harley MS 3528, ff.11v–21:** 'Compendium utile vel Rosarius' [in a later hand 'Toletani Philosophi'], 15th cent., in Latin (DWS 231 xiv)

**Sloane MS 212, ff.99v–120v:** 15th cent., in Latin (DWS 231 xv)

**Sloane MS 2476, ff.11–39:** in a later hand 'Dastin Rosarium secretissimum philosophorum arcanum comprehendens' 15th cent., in Latin (DWS 231 xvi)

**Sloane MS 3744, ff.35–37:** (extract) 15th cent., in Latin (DWS 231 xvii)

**Stowe MS 1070, ff. ff.42–43v:** (extract) 15th cent., in Latin (DWS 231 xviii)

*Rosarius* or *Liber abbreviatus*
incipit: 'Iste namque liber vocatur Roarius' (TK 793) (DWS 233)

**Additional MS 10,764, ff.22v–42v:** 15th cent., in Latin (DWS 233 iii)

**Sloane MS 2325, ff.22–39:** 'Rosarius' 15th cent., in Latin (DWS 233 iv)

**Stowe MS 1070, ff.38–39:** compilation from *Rosarius*, 15th cent., in Latin (DWS 234)

*Theorica et practica* (whole or excerpts)
incipit (of dedication): 'Venerande pater gratias [ago] deo' (TK 1683), (DWS 226) or 'Reverende pater gratias ago deo qui istam scientiam' (TK 1355)

**Additional MS 10,764, ff.71–74:** 'Incipit Epistola Magistri Anraldi de villa nova . . . ad papam Bonefacium de lapide philosophorum' 15th cent., in Latin (DWS 226 viii)

**Additional MS 10,764, ff.157–163:** 'Incipit theorica et practica magistri arnaldi de villa nova ad sanctissimum patrem' 15th cent., in Latin (DWS 226 ix)

**Additional MS 15,549, ff.110–121v:** f.121v: 'Explicit liber nude veritate in hac arte' 15th cent., in Latin (DWS 226 x)

**Harley MS 3703, ff.25–30:** explicit f.30: 'Explicit tractatus qui dicitur venerande patre', 14th cent., in Latin (DWS 226 i)

**Sloane MS 276, ff.77v–79:** 15th cent., in Latin (DWS 226 xii)

**Sloane MS 276, ff.79v–82:** 15th cent., in Latin (DWS 226 xiii)

**Sloane MS 630, ff.98–115:** 'Practica Arnaldi de Villa nova', 17th cent., in English

**Sloane MS 692, ff.94v–96v:** 15th cent., in Latin (DWS 226 xiv)

**Sloane MS 1091, ff.164–165v:** 15th cent., (excerpt) in Latin (DWS 226 xv)

**Sloane MS 1698, ff.58–62v:** 15th cent., in Latin (DWS Corr 226 xva)

**Sloane MS 2479, ff.77–80v:** (excerpt) 'Theorica alkanamie [sic] Arnoldi de Villa nova' 14th cent., in Latin (DWS 226 ii)

*Tractatus notabilis in arte majori*
incipit (to introduction): 'In nomine sancte et individue trinitatis partis et filii et spiritus sancti. Amen.'
incipit: (to prefatory verses) 'In principio ponemus aliquos versus in quibus tota patebit' (TK 713), DWS 228)

**Additional MS 10,764, ff.77–84v:** 15th cent., in Latin (DWS 228 i)

**Harley MS 5403, ff.43–50v:** 'Liber de compositione medicinae sive elixiris' written 1410 (see f.50v): 15th cent., in Latin (DWS 228 ii)

**Sloane MS 3457, ff. 434v–447:** 15th cent., in Latin (DWS 228 iii)

*Others*

**Sloane MS 320, ff.33v–34v:** 'Notes gathered owt of the Testament of Arnaldus Philosophicus', 16th cent., in English

# Thomas Norton

*The ordinal of alchemy*
incipit of introduction: 'Liber iste clericalis monstrat scientiam'
incipit of work: 'To the honour of god one in persons thre / This booke is made that lay men should it see' (DWS 814)

**Additional MS 10,302, ff.1–67:** 15th cent., in English (DWS 814 i)

**Harley MS 853, ff.26v–65:** 16th cent., in English

**Royal MS 18 B. XXIV, ff.79–139:** 'Thomas norton of Alchymy', f.79v Latin verses in praise of the book by Walter Haddon, Master of Trinity Hall, Cambridge, 16th cent., in English;

**Sloane MS 1198, ff.1–39v:** 16th cent., in English

**Sloane MS 1751, ff.17–72v:** 16th cent., in English

**Sloane MS 1873, ff.3–84:** 16th cent., in English

**Sloane MS 2174, ff.89–116v:** 'A book of Alchymy in verse in old English', 17th cent., in English

**Sloane MS 2203, ff.91–97v:** an abridgement by Sir H Platt, 17th cent., in English

Sloane MS 2532, ff.1–50: 'The Bouke of Thomas Norton', 16th cent., in English

Sloane MS 3580B, ff.60v–118v: 'The secret ordinall of Alchimy, A scyence moste excellent & holy', copied out 1580 (see f.117), 16th cent., in English

Sloane MS 2036, ff.30–36v: (extracts), 16th cent., in English

## Thomas Charnock

*Breviary of natural philosophy*
incipit: 'The Book speaketh . . . "Come hither my children of this discipline"'

Sloane MS 684, ff.1–23v: 'Anno domini, a thowsande v. hunderyth fyftye & vii / alle lawde and prease, be unto god in heaven / beinge the friste frydaye of the new yere / I was then begoun, as here after shalle appere', 16th cent., in English

Sloane MS 2194, ff.48–56: 'Jhesus. A Booke named the Breviary of Philosophie compiled by the unlettered Scholler Thomas Charnocke studious in the most worthie Science of Astronomie & Philosophie. Anno Domini 1557 1° januarii & excriptum 28 martii 1601', written 1601, 17th cent., in English

'A Booke Dedicated to the Queenes majestie'
Lansdowne MS 703, ff.1–53: a holograph copy in Charnock's hand, dated from his house in Stockland Bristol November 1565. Lord Burleigh's autograph is on f.1

A parchment roll containing 'Lullian' alchemical diagrams and wheels, and drawings of alchemical vessels.

Sloane MS 2640: 16th cent., in English and Latin. A note at the foot of the roll, now largely illegible on the MS reads as follows in the transciption in the Sloane catalogue: 'Thomas Charnock of Stokeland, Bristow, who travelled all the realm of England over for to obtain unto the secrets of this science, which, as God would, he did attain unto, anno Domini 1555; as it appeareth more plainly in the Book which I dedicated unto Queen Elizabeth of England. Born at Feversham in Kent, 1526'.

# INDEX